Brother Man, Sister Girl: Volume 1

Copyright © Shakirah Green
ISBN: 978-1-958186-01-5
LOC: 2022938690

Publisher, Editor and Book Design:
Fiery Beacon Publishing House, LLC
Fiery Beacon Consulting and Publishing Group

Graphics: FBPH Graphics Team, Dashona Smith

This work was produced in Greensboro, North Carolina, United States of America. All rights reserved under International Copyright Law.

The contents of this work are not necessarily the views of Fiery Beacon Publishing House, LLC nor any of its affiliates. No portion of this publication may be reproduced, stored in any electronic system, or transmitted in any form or by any means (electronic, mechanical, photocopy, recording or otherwise) without written permission from Shakirah Green and/or Fiery Beacon Publishing House, LLC. All individual authors in this work own copyright to their chapter only. Brief quotations may be used in literary reviews.

Brother *Man*

Sister *Girl*

Shakirah Green

Table Of Contents

Dedication

Introduction   6

Chapter 1	The Disturbance	10
Chapter 2	An Invasion of Privacy	26
Chapter 3	The Morning After	54
Chapter 4	Life Or Death	72
Chapter 5	The Confrontation	83
Chapter 6	Believe It Or Not	114
Chapter 7	The Discovery	135
Chapter 8	The Intruder	141

About the Author   162

Dedication

There's nothing more rewarding than to finally accomplish a dream, a goal, and have someone believe in you every step of the way. Because of the appreciation and the testimonials of those who read "Call A Spade A Spade" and for those who were intrigued enough to persuade me to continue writing, I dedicate "Brother Man Sister Girl" to you. It is because of you that this book has been written. Thank You for investing in me.

- Author Shakirah Green

Introduction

Gazing into Brother Man's eyes, Sister Girl couldn't help but feel the passion that aggressively flowed between them. Her heart began to palpitate. Her hands became more sweaty than usual. She was engulfed with the sweet enchantment of the evening. Her surroundings became non-existent.

No noise.

No hustle or bustle of those nearby.

No city lights.

All she saw was him.

All she wanted was him.

All she needed was him.

She loved him.

As Brother Man continued to wait patiently for her response, and her lips partially parted to give an answer, she couldn't help but pause and reminisce about her past experience. In her past relationship, Sister Girl was presented with the same offer as Brother Man had just given, not knowing that the relationship would end in abuse. Naïve and believing it was love, she accepted the offer presented from her former. She knew what the outcome would be if she accepted but, weak in her flesh, she yielded. At her acceptance, her life changed, and she experienced a whirl of hurt, embarrassment, and unforgettable pain. She gave in to the temptation of fornication and conceived a child. She was saved, sanctified, and living for the Lord. *"How could I have done this? Why did I allow this to happen? What in the world was I thinking? This is unforgivable. I'm such a failure,"* were the words of her past that echoed in her soul.

Young, depressed and confused, she decided to have an abortion. Her guilt and shame began to affect her performance at work, she lost her job, and gloom began to interfere with her relationship with family and friends. She was released from the Praise and Worship team and all auxiliaries at her former church. She became anti-social and suicidal due to the abuse she was experiencing throughout the entire relationship. At that very moment, while contemplating her response to Brother Man, she remembered what her mother always told her after that incident, "Now that you are forgiven, stay forgiven. Keep your standards and refuse to open the door."

With tears in her eyes, she looked at her fiancé and said, "I can't. I can't stay." Brother Man looked at Sister Girl with deep affection, wiped her tears while tears of his own fell from his eyes, kissed her gently yet passionately and said,

"I still love you. It was only a test of your standards. Now I know for certain, you were meant for me."

-1-

The Disturbance

The morning after was filled with so much anticipation. How is it possible that someone else's joy could become so tangible that it begins to ring out to others? It was like a dream. All she could do was reminiscence about last night. Sister Girl's childhood dream is finally coming true. No more wishing and hoping upon a star. Her Mr. Right has found her, and now she's headed down the road of wedded bliss. Everything in her life seemed right. She has her dream career, her dream car, and now her dream man. She truly believed that nothing, absolutely nothing, could go wrong. She was living in the clouds at this point, and no one could convince her to come down.

As Sister Girl continued to lay in her queen size bed, under her pink plush comforter, she hugged her pillow tightly as if to hug her man. She closed her eyes and replayed the night before over and over in her mind. The night was enchanting. It was perfect. The ambience, the poetry, the fantasy coach ride, and the gifts made the entire evening complete. She's getting married! Tears began to stream down her face as she pictured Brother Man kneeling before her to ask one of the most memorable questions that a woman could ever be asked. As she sat on the edge of the bed, she began to stare at her diamond cut engagement ring. Immediately, excitement filled her heart, so much so that she jumped up and screamed, "Oh my God, I'm getting married!" She could care less if she woke up her neighbors in her townhouse community. She could care less if she was disturbing the peace. She could care less that it was 6:30 am on a Saturday morning when everyone was probably still sleeping from a hard work week. She was getting married, and she wanted the world to know.

Sister Girl slid her feet into her cozy pink furry bedroom slippers, put on her pink silk house robe, and was headed to the kitchen. She wanted to start her own celebration by cooking an early morning full-course breakfast. Right before she entered the kitchen, she turned on her surround sound stereo and turned the volume up to almost blasting. She went through her playlist and decided to listen to some old school music, the song "Celebration" to be exact. As soon as she heard the beat drop, she started dancing around the room. Jumping up and down, hopping and skipping with the biggest smile on her face. She was fully engaged in the moment. She grabbed the broom and made it her personal microphone stand, singing "Ceee-le-bra-tion," at the top of her lungs. She felt like a little girl all over again.

With the music playing and happiness filling the air, she made her way to the kitchen. "I know I shouldn't, but I'm gon' do it anyway." She opened the refrigerator and grabbed the eggs, sausage, bacon, butter, cheese, biscuits, orange juice, and milk. She closed the refrigerator and went to the kitchen cabinet. She grabbed the box of instant grits and all of her seasonings. "Wait. I almost forgot." She went to the freezer and grabbed the hashbrowns and premade pancakes. She set her cappuccino maker to make a cup of sweet hazelnut. As she began to cook her breakfast feast, the delicious aroma filled the house. She looked at the amount of food she was preparing and started having second thoughts. "Maybe I shouldn't eat all of this food." When every bride-to-be thinks about the amount of weight she could lose before her wedding day, she begins a ridiculous diet to shed those extra pounds. The bride absolutely must look fabulous in her gown. But, right now, Sister Girl wanted to celebrate with food. "Nah. I'll start my diet tomorrow." As she continued to cook and sing loudly with the song that she had on repeat, there was a knock at the door. Unfortunately, Sister Girl didn't hear the knock because the music was so loud. "Ceee-le-bra-tion." There was another knock at the door. This time, she paused because she believed she heard something, but she didn't pause long enough to hear it again. So, she continued. The third time, the knocks were louder and more forceful as if it was a police officer banging down the door.

She grabbed the stereo remote from the front right-side pocket of her robe and turned down the music. "Who is it?," she asked as she approached the front door of her townhouse.

With obvious frustration in her voice, "Gem," the woman replied. Gem is Sister Girl's neighbor, and an obnoxious and nosy one. Sister Girl squinted through the peep hole in the door, and Gem was not happy. Sister Girl took a deep breath, said to herself "be nice" and reluctantly opened the door because she anticipated what Gem was going to say. Standing there was Gem, with her cucumber facial mask applied, her leopard-printed house robe, pearl earrings and matching necklace, and expensive three-inch heel house slippers. Gem was considered "the town's spoiled brat," and she had no problem accepting that title. She knew it was true, and she loved it. Her father was one of the best district attorneys in the state and he, like his daughter, had no problem flaunting. Her father made sure she had everything her heart desired no matter the cost. She spoke the word, and it was hers without debate or conversation. If she wanted it, her father made it happen.

"Good morning, Gem," Sister Girl greeted softly. "Umm, do you have any idea what time it is, Little Girl?," said Gem snobbishly. After taking another deep breath, "my name is Sister Girl, Gem," she said respectfully while holding back her tongue, "and no, I'm not aware of the time." She really didn't care what time it was, honestly because she was enjoying the fact that she was getting married. She'd been through so much in her life, but now she was able to experience true love, real love. "Well, if you weren't so busy making noise and sounding like a drunk canary, you would realize that you're disturbing my peace." Gem tossed her head back to whip her long hair behind her shoulder. Sister Girl wanted to slam the door in her face so badly but, if she did, she wouldn't be a good representative of a Christian woman, but, oh did she want to. She could if she had an excuse to slam the door. At that very moment, as if God answered her prayer, the smoke alarm went off in the kitchen. She had completely forgotten about her celebration breakfast feast. Yes! This was the perfect opportunity. "Sorry. Gotta go!."

    She slammed the door in Gem's face and ran to the kitchen. Slamming the door was such a gratifying feeling to her. She wasn't sure if she should feel that happy about being so rude, but the smile on her face was undeniable. When she got to the stove, she discovered that only the bacon was burnt. Thankfully, there was bacon left in the package to cook for her feast. She turned on the exhaust fan above the stove to vent some of the smoke that accumulated. She placed the remaining bacon in the skillet on medium. Suddenly, there was a knock at the door, but since the fan was blowing, she couldn't hear the knock. A few moments later, there was another knock at the door. Just as before, Sister Girl believed she heard the knock but wasn't quite sure. Instead of ignoring the knock this time, she decided to answer. She turned off the fan above the stove, walked through the formal dining room, which was adorned with golden Victorian décor, and approached the front door. Once again, Sister Girl looked through the peep hole and sighed. There stood Gem as angry as a Pitbull. "Are you kidding me?," Sister Girl said to herself. She opened the door, hoping and praying that she didn't have to be rude to her neighbor again. Infuriated, Gem continued her rant. "You call yourself a Christian?! You are so ultimately rude! How dare you slam the door in my face?! Who do you think you are?! Do you not know who I am?!" Sister Girl replied very calmly, "Would you rather have my kitchen burn down while being disrespected?" Just when she thought that Gem had reached the peak of her temper tantrum, she replied, "Disrespected?! What do you mean 'disrespected'?! I didn't disrespect you, Little Girl. Every word that was spoken was true. You do sound like a drunk canary, and obviously you can't cook." Sister Girl dropped her head and, yet again, took a deep breath. "Yup. I'm gonna do it," she said to herself. As if to say "Bye, Bye," Sister Girl looked at Gem with a fake smile, cocked her head to the side and slammed the door harder than the slam before. She walked away dusting her hands and said to herself, "I may be wrong Lord, but man that felt good."

She ran back to the kitchen to finish cooking her breakfast feast. Thankfully, there was no burnt food this time. While she was preparing her place setting at the dining room table, Sister Girl could not help but wonder what came over Gem that she would be that disrespectful to her. Sure, they've had their moments of disagreement but never to this magnitude. Quite honestly, Gem seemed to have acted a little stranger than normal. Whatever it was, Sister Girl prayed that Gem would get her act together quickly, especially if she had any plans on knocking at her door again.

After all of the commotion this morning, Sister Girl was finally able to sit down at her place setting and enjoy her celebratory breakfast feast. As soon as she placed her fork into her cheesy grits, there was a knock at the door. "Uggh! Are you kidding me?" She dropped her fork into her plate. "What in the world?," Sister Girl said out of frustration. "Lord are you telling me to fast or something because this doesn't make any sense. Your daughter is hungry, and this woman keeps bothering me." While she was venting, there was another knock at the door. By this time, Sister Girl was fed up with the games that Gem was pulling. She approached the door but, this time, didn't look through the peep hole. She already knew it was Gem trying to get under her skin again. She yanked the door open while yelling, "What?!" "Dang girl, calm down." It wasn't Gem at all. It was a few of her close friends from college. Sister Girl's mouth dropped open to her chest. She was frozen in shock. She didn't know what to say. She wanted to apologize but she was so surprised that there were no words spoken. So, instead, she began to cry.

These friends were more like sisters to Sister Girl. They all met during their freshman year of college in Detroit. At that time, they were all new to the city and had absolutely no idea where to go, what to do or who to ask. So, here are four strangers bonded into a sisterhood, and fifteen years later that sisterhood hadn't been broken. They were there for each other during hook-ups, break-ups, birthdays, marriages, pregnancies, and even the deaths of loved ones. They shared the good, the bad and the ugly moments together. Nothing could break their love for each other. "Oh my God! When? How? Oh my God!" Sister Girl was still standing there in the doorway trying to get her words together. They looked at each other, and the four began to cry. It had been a minute since they were together. Suddenly, a burst of happiness filled their hearts. They all began to scream in excitement, hugging each other in a long-lasting embrace. While in their love huddle, Coco said "Umm, has anyone noticed that we still standing *outside* in *front* of the house instead of standing *inside* of the house?" They all chuckled as Sister Girl invited them inside. "What? I'm just saying." Coco was one of the four sisters that had a spontaneous, hilarious, and charismatic nature, but she also had a way with words, and her behavior may shift if anyone approached her or her sisters incorrectly. "Wow sis, you have a beautiful home," Ivory said as they entered. Ivory was more polite, passive, and soft spoken of the four. She was the main one that had to be dragged to any type of campus event because she didn't think she fit in with the rest of the girls. "Thank you so much. I've lived here for about four years now. The gardens are so beautiful, and it's very peaceful here except for one person."

As soon as Sister Girl completed her comment, there was a knock at the door. Sister Girl deliberately ignored the knock because she didn't want anything disturbing the reunion with her sisters. However, the knocks kept coming. "You want me to answer it, sis?" Coco asked, noticing that her sister was showing signs of "I'm over it." Sister Girl gave her the nod, not caring who was at the door. She knew that if it was you-know-who, it was going to be trouble. Coco opened the door. Screaming to the top of her lungs was Gem, with her fists balled up near her head suggesting that she has a major headache due to their excitement. "Why don't you shut up?!! It's eight o'clock in the morning!" While Gem continued screaming disrespectful comments to Sister Girl and her guests, Coco looked at her and slammed the door. Sister Girl immediately burst out laughing. "Why are you laughing so hard sis?," Ivory wanted to know. "Hopefully, after having the door slammed in her face for the third time today, she would know not to come back over here," Sister Girl replied. "Dang, three times? That's craziness," Candy said. Candy was the oldest of the four sisters. She was always in "chill mode." She didn't allow too much of the drama, confrontation, and foolishness to bother her. Her smooth demeanor, however, had been mistaken for weakness many times. Individuals who attempted to test her weakness quickly discovered that she's a "quiet storm". Candy walked to the window near the doorway, drew back the silk drapery, and witnessed Gem walking away from Sister Girl's property. "Well, there she goes," Candy said. Ivory also witnessed Gem leaving Sister Girl's front lawn, however, to Ivory, something wasn't right about Gem's body language. Usually, if a person is highly upset about something and walking away from a dramatic scene, the individual walks away quite rapidly and perhaps stumping away in a tantrum. For a person that just had the door slammed in her face three times in one morning, you would expect her to be furious, but not Gem. Her body language was calm, no fast paced or stomping away, just calm, too calm if you'd ask Ivory. Right before Ivory left the window, she noticed that Gem turned around and stared at Sister Girl's house in a creepy and cold way and then proceeded to her own house next door. This did not sit well with Ivory at all.

"Hey sis? How long have you been neighbors with the "disturbed" woman that was at your door? There's something about her that's off, almost like she's capable of doing something stupid. I'm definitely not picking up good vibes from her at all. Do you feel safe around her?," Ivory asked with deep concern. "I'm good sis. Thanks for caring," Sister Girl replied. "She's been acting the same way since I moved to this neighborhood. She's disrespectful when she wants to move people out of 'her' neighborhood. For some reason, she believes she owns people because her dad is wealthy and well-known. She's 'Little Miss Princess' to her father, but around here she's known as 'the town's spoiled brat'." "She crazy, that's for sure, but she ain't crazy enough to try something at this address. I can bet you that much. She better not come over here starting nothing, or she's gonna find out real quick who's crazy for real," Coco said, ending her speech in a karate pose. "Girl, something is wrong with you. I told y'all that something was wrong with Coco when we saw her wondering around campus talking to herself," Sister Girl said. Everybody immediately started laughing remembering the very moment that Sister Girl mentioned. Coco, in excitement said, "Hurry up sis! Go get dressed! It's time for us to do what we do best!" "Pray?," Ivory asked while chuckling to herself.

She already knew what the girls were about to say. "Ivory...," Coco was about to finish her sentence when Ivory interrupted with a smile on her face. "I know. I know. Go stand in the corner." Everyone started laughing again but, what's funnier was that she actually went to the corner of the living room and stood there. They couldn't believe it. She was coming out of that "I don't fit" shell. She actually made them laugh. Ivory was now officially a part of The Phenomenal Four. After that laugh, Sister Girl ran to her room to prepare for a day out with the girls.

Music blasting the 90's jams - Black BMW sparkling - cash flowing - The Phenomenal Four looked and smelled amazing. They were ready to enjoy whatever excitement that the day had in store for them. This day was well overdue, and Sister Girl was going to embrace every moment. Since the BMW was Candy's vehicle, she drove and Sister Girl rode "shot gun." "So, bride-to-be, where to?," Candy asked. "Please say we going to get something to eat,'cause yo' sister is *hangry*." Now you know that those words could only come out of one mouth. Yup, Coco. Sister Girl agreed while laughing. "Yes, we're going to get something to eat." "Hallelujah!" Coco shouted from the back seat, making "shouting" music, and clapping her hands as if she's going to Pentecost. Sister Girl continued explaining her day to the girls. "After being interrupted by Gem all morning, I couldn't enjoy the celebration breakfast feast that I prepared for myself. She kept coming over complaining about everything and was very disrespectful. Maybe I was wrong for being so loud this morning, but I think she was just over exaggerating when she said that I was 'disturbing her peace.' Anyhew, I'm just glad to be with my besties." Sister Girl's eyes began to tear. "Nu-uh! None of that 'huntey.' You gon' mess up your make-up. Now where we going to get something to eat? My stomach speaking in tongues.," Coco said. "Why don't we go to our spot? You know the place where the waiters are all men dressed like Firemen and come to your tables with no shirts on. Whooo, I can see it already." Coco started reminiscing while the words were being formed in her mind. "Coco, they had to close that restaurant down because the waiters were complaining of sexual harassment." They all started laughing. Barely able to catch her breath, Candy added, "It was Coco's fault. She started it!"

In that moment, the sisters didn't want to be anywhere else but with each other. They finally agreed to enjoy Japanese cuisine, which was a longtime favorite. They made reservations for 3:00 pm at a terrific restaurant downtown where one can enjoy fine dining, the best picks of wine, and a great view of the city - the beautiful setting of downtown Los Angeles. "I wonder if there's any fine Japanese men down there," Coco said. Everyone looked at her, chuckled and shook their heads. "What? Foreigners need loving too." Ivory smiled, but she really wasn't focused on the comedy that was happening inside the car. She couldn't put her finger on it, but something just didn't feel right. She kept replaying the mischievous smirk that was on Gem's face as she walked off Sister Girl's property. "What's wrong boo?," Candy asked Ivory as she looked into the rear-view mirror. "Ivory?" "Huh?" "What's wrong?," Candy asked again. Everyone became concerned. Ivory has always been somewhat of a quiet one, however, this type of quietness was abnormal. "I'm…ummm…I'm okay. I just can't shake this weird feeling about Gem. I'm trying. I really am, but something isn't right. I can feel it." "Girl, stop being paranoid and enjoy yourself. We've waited so long for this moment to be together. Don't let some uppity rich girl steal this," Candy said. "If you ain't straight by the time we get to this restaurant, you know where you going right?," Coco asked her. "In the corner," Ivory said with a smile on her face. She took a deep breath. "Okay, okay. I'm good!" Ivory said it out of her mouth but, inwardly, she wasn't good at all.

Around 5:00 pm, while The Phenomenal Four were enjoying their night on the town, Sister Girl's mother was flying into Los Angeles from Philadelphia to surprise her. Momma had to be there for her daughter to make sure that her head wasn't still stuck in the clouds. She knew her daughter very well. Sister Girl would be so lost in the hype of being engaged that she would forget to start planning the wedding, and Momma couldn't let that happen to her little girl. She knew that the girls were going to be out celebrating because she planned it that way - sneaky. She quickly sent a text message to Candy to inform her of her arrival. Since Momma already had a key to Sister Girl's home, she asked airport transportation to drive her to her daughter's home. Momma was so excited. She couldn't wait to see the expression on Sister Girl's face. After about forty-five minutes of sight-seeing, Momma finally arrived at the house. She always traveled light, so there wasn't a lot of luggage to retrieve from the trunk of the vehicle. The transportation attendant took the liberty in helping Momma with her two-piece Louis Vuitton luggage set and escorted her to the front door. She thanked him and blessed him generously. She located the house keys in her purse and unlocked the door. Once the driver noticed Momma unlocking the door, he drove away.

As she opened the front door, she noticed that Sister Girl had remodeled her home beautifully. She loved the Victorian themed décor. "My baby's so talented," Momma said to herself while a warmth filled her heart. She turned around, bent down, and grabbed her luggage from the doorway to place it inside. All of a sudden, when Momma stood up, there was a mysterious looking woman standing at the edge of the street in front of the driveway. The look on the woman's face was chilling. Momma threw her luggage in the house, quickly closed the door, locked it, and ran to the front window. In her state of fear, she slowly peeped through the curtain only to notice that the woman was still standing there staring at the house, wearing a black pull-over hoodie, black pants, and black boots. Momma immediately closed the curtain and stepped away from the window. Attempting to control her heart rate, she began to take deep breaths. "In through the nose - out through the mouth," she repeated the cycle to herself. A few seconds had passed, and her heart rate had stabilized, so Momma decided to take one last peep to see if the "woman in black" was still there. Once again, she slowly approached the front window and slightly opened the curtain. The woman was gone. She had no idea who it was and, quite frankly, didn't care to know either. Momma was just glad that the woman wasn't there - creepy. The thought of her staring at the house began to affect Momma's heart rate all over again. In through the nose - out through the mouth. She repeated her breathing techniques for two additional cycles while proceeding to the guest room with her belongings, praying in the hallway — "I plead the Blood over this house and over that crazy woman."

-2-

An Invasion of Privacy

As soon as she reached the room, her cell phone unexpectantly began to vibrate. Startled, Momma flinched and let out a little squeal. She began to chuckle to herself. "There's no reason to be scared. Get yourself together." Ashamed of herself, she shook her head as she reached into the side pocket of her cashmere sweater to get her phone. It was a text message notification from Candy. *"I got your message. We'll be there around 8."* Momma replied "OK" to the text message and looked at the time displayed on her phone. It was already 6:30 pm. "Oh my goodness. I've got to hurry up." Momma wanted to purchase Sister Girl's slumber party favorites, just as she did when her daughter was younger. Swiftly, Momma unpacked her luggage and headed to the kitchen to take an inventory of what she needed to purchase. When she got to the kitchen, her mouth dropped. It was a mess! "What in the world?!" There were pots and pans all over the place. Sister Girl hadn't cleaned the kitchen after she prepared the Celebration Breakfast Feast that she never got a chance to eat due to the unwanted visitations of her neighbor.

Momma became a little disappointed with Sister Girl. "She knows better than this," Momma said, clueless of what her daughter had to endure during the day. There was no time for the "mommy moment" though. Momma had to become as lightening in order to clean up the kitchen, go to the store and return before the girls get back from their shenanigans. She managed to clean the kitchen in approximately thirty minutes. Momma was a little winded, but her cleaning mission was accomplished. "Now, let me think. Where does she leave the spare key to her car?" Sister Girl told Momma once before but now, in her sense of urgency, Momma couldn't remember. She searched every vase and side table in the house; she even looked inside of the entertainment center. "If I were a key, where would I be?," she asked herself. She stood still for a moment hoping to get revelation of the next place to look, but nothing came to her mind. Anxious to leave, Momma started looking for the spare key in places that made no sense to look, like in the kitchen cabinets and in the bathroom. "Little key? Where are you little key?," she sang as if the key had ears. Of course, the key never responded. So, in frustration, Momma got to Sister Girl's room and flopped onto her bed.

It was a little dim in the room, so Momma decided to turn on the lamp on the nightstand. Then, she remembered. She lifted the lamp - TADA! She found the key underneath the base of the lampstand! "YES!," Momma shouted as she ran to the guest room, grabbed her MK handbag and ran to the front door. She turned around to make sure that all the lights in the house were off and locked the top and bottom locks behind her. Even though Sister Girl lived in a nice and safe neighborhood, one can never be too careful. Momma unlocked the driver side door of Sister Girl's pearl-white Mercedes Benz and jumped in. She buckled her seatbelt, adjusted the rear-view mirror, and put the car in reverse. Momma had less than an hour to run her errand and be back to the house to surprise Sister Girl. As she cautiously pulled out of the driveway, she looked into the rear-view mirror to make sure she was in the clear. "Ahhh!" Momma immediately slammed on the brakes, bringing the car to an abrupt stop. She turned around to look out of the back window, but she was gone. "She was right there." The "woman in black" was standing at the end of the driveway again but, by the time Momma stopped the car to look behind her, she was gone. IN THROUGH THE NOSE - OUT THROUGH THE MOUTH. Anyone at this moment would stop and think they're going insane, but Momma had no time to stop; she had to get going. So, she drove off, constantly looking in the rear-view mirror. "I'm not crazy. I'm not crazy," she continued to affirm to herself as she headed to the grocery store.

It's 7:55 pm and, after dashing in and out of traffic and speed walking through the store to find her daughter's favorites, Momma finally made it back to Sister Girl's home.

As she pulled into the driveway, she noticed that the lights were turned on inside the house. She looked around but didn't see Candy's BMW, which let her know that she arrived before the girls were back from their night out. Puzzled, Momma sat in the car for a few seconds trying to recall her steps. "Now, I know I turned off these lights before I left." Momma wrapped the plastic grocery bag around her forearm, grabbed her belongings and stepped out of the vehicle. She surveyed her surroundings to see if she could identify anyone around, but there was no disturbance at all. There was no one walking, no one driving. It was quiet. Almost too quiet. Momma walked to the front door to check the doorknob. It was still locked. Momma's confusion increased to a whole different level. She was 100% sure that she turned off the lights before she left. If no one was home, how could the doorknob still be locked with the lights turned on inside? Realizing that she had been standing outside for a few moments, she decided to find the key to unlock the door. As she was looking through her handbag, The Phenomenal Four was pulling into the driveway. "That looks like my mom!," Sister Girl said with excitement. "SURPRISE!," the girls all shouted. "Oh, my goodness! Y'all knew about this?" "Yup!," Candy replied.

Sister Girl could hardly wait to hug and kiss her mother. As soon as Candy parked the car, Sister Girl jumped out of the BMW and ran towards her mother. Momma was rushing to place the grocery bag of goodies into the house before Sister Girl had a chance to see the surprises she purchased. Momma finally unlocked and opened the front door, but not before Sister Girl reached her mother and witnessed what her eyes beheld. They both stood there in the doorway, frozen in disbelief. Speechless. After getting out of the car, Ivory looked at Candy and Coco and said, "Something isn't right." Momma's arms and hands became numb, dropping the grocery bag and her handbag to the ground. Sister Girl's eyes began to form tears of shock and anger. When Ivory, Coco and Candy approached the front door, they were confused as to why Momma and Sister Girl looked like statues. Then, the wave of emotion engulfed the three of them as they viewed the reason why Momma and Sister Girl were frozen. A time that was supposed to be filled with love and laughter had now shifted to a time of confusion and anger.

Sister Girl slowly stepped over the threshold of the doorway as the others followed. "Why?!," Sister Girl screamed with tears flowing down her cheeks. She paused again as she slowly glanced over the chaos. "Who would do this?" she said sadly. She finally gained the strength to walk further into her living room area that laid in ruin. Tears continued to flow as she realized that everything that was destroyed were priceless items that were memories of love. Nothing material, like her surround sound stereo or entertainment center, were damaged in any way. However, pictures of her and her mother and father at her college graduation ceremony were scratched severely, as if someone had somewhat of a flashback and used a sharp object to scratch out their faces. She moved further into the house and noticed that one of the most precious pictures of her love had been stripped into pieces. The memory was lodged into her mind - unforgettable. It didn't matter that the photo was retrievable in her mobile phone. Shredding the picture of her and Brother Man holding each other on the night of their engagement was as if it was a personal message to her. It seemed like those things that were close to her heart were the things destroyed, but who would take the time to hurt her this way? Sister Girl was, for the most part, a quiet woman. She always found a way to keep peace in the midst of any confrontational situation and to her knowledge, she hadn't made any enemies with anyone. Everyone at work, church, even business owners that knew her in the marketplace only had positive comments to say about her character, so, to Sister Girl, it just didn't make sense. Who would go through these lengths to show such hatred?

She took a deep breath, patted her eyes to rid them of tears, and headed to her bedroom to see if any damage was done. As she entered her room, she noticed that everything was as she had left it. Sister Girl began to think to herself, "Why only destroy the things in the living room and not in my room?" She sat down on the bed and began to ponder the many thoughts that were running through her mind. "Who?" and "Why?" were the two major questions. After a few moments, she stood and headed into the hallway to join her Momma and her besties in the living room. As she walked through the hallway, she had the urge to turn around and head back to her bedroom. Something just didn't sit well with her. Her room was perfectly fine, but there was a turning in her stomach, so she had to find out what was leading her back to the room.

When she walked back into the bedroom, she slowly looked around to see if anything was out of place. Her personal belongings, her jewelry, her 55-inch flatscreen Smart TV - everything was fine; even her picture frames were still in the same place as usual on her nightstands.

Wait.

Why were the pictures in the front room destroyed and not the ones in her room? Sister Girl walked to the nightstand facing the entrance of her bedroom door and picked up the picture frame. The picture frame was not damaged at all, but the picture was sliced with precision and placed back into the frame. It was a picture of her and Brother Man on their very first date. Sister Girl's face had been carefully carved out, and her dress was slashed. Suddenly, anger was matched with fear as Sister Girl walked to the other nightstand to observe the other picture, which was a memory of her and Brother Man's first kiss. Just as the other, her face was carved completely out, her dress slashed, and the photo was placed back into the frame.

Sister Girl's pace of breathing increased, almost to the point of hyperventilation. She was about to lose it. "Breathe girl," she said to herself. "Breathe." Inhale - Exhale. She sat on the edge of the bed for a few more moments until she finally decided to get up and join her guests. On the way out of the room, she walked to the closet to change from her stiletto heels into her favorite pink fuzzy bedroom slippers. When she opened the closet doors, she noticed that her clothing seemed to have been shuffled around. Sister Girl always arranged her closet according to clothing type and color. So, she immediately noticed that a few of her blouses were now mixed-in with her summer dresses, and her formal wear was now mingling in with her business attire. She continued to look closer at the disarray.

"OH MY GOD!!"

"What happened?!," Momma shouted anxiously from the living room. "I can't believe this!," Sister Girl shouted. Instantly, Momma, Coco, Ivory, and Candy came running down the hallway to meet Sister Girl in her bedroom. "What?! What's going on?!," shouted Coco. "They're gone. Both of them are gone.," Sister Girl said in fear. "What's gone?," Momma asked. "I know what I have hanging in my closet at all times. I know every piece of clothing that I own, and they both are gone." "What's gone, girl?!," Coco asked again frantically. Sister Girl pointed to the pictures that were on her nightstands. Coco grabbed the frame from the nightstand facing the bedroom door, and Candy grabbed the other from the far-side of the room. "Oh my God," Candy said in disbelief, "Who would do something like this?" Sister Girl said as she hung her head low, "They're both gone." The dresses that were slashed in the pictures were now missing from her closet. In shock, they all stood there with their mouths gapped open speechless as to what to say next as they gazed into her closet. How...What...When...Huh? As if Momma didn't believe her daughter, she rushed to Sister Girl's closet and noticed that the dresses were missing. "Maybe you put them in the cleaners and forgot to pick them up," Momma suggested. "No, Momma. I had them dry-cleaned last week because I was planning to wear one of them to our engagement party next weekend. I couldn't decide which dress, so I decided to get both of them dry-cleaned and pressed."

Sister Girl began to cry and flopped down on the bed. Ivory's eyes began to tear as she sat down beside her on the edge of the bed. "I called the police while you were in here. They should be here shortly. We'll figure this mess out. Don't you worry. Everything will be ok." Ivory gently wiped Sister Girl's tears and gave her a warm embrace. "Have you called your fiancé to let him know what happened?," Candy asked. "No, not yet. Honestly, I'm really hesitant in calling him. If he finds out what happened, he'll want me to move in with him and that will ruin everything. I had my engagement party, and everything all planned out. This isn't how it's supposed to be." Sister Girl explained while her heart ached in devastation. Momma sat down on the other side of Sister Girl, held her hand and looked into her eyes. "Sweetheart, listen. I know that this is supposed to be a very special moment in your life. I know that you've been waiting for a long time to experience this magnitude of love. What has happened here is terrible and trust me, we're gonna get to the bottom of this, but, despite the chaos, don't allow it to destroy the opportunity you have to live your life with your true love. Brother Man loves you. I can see it in his eyes. I'm sure he would want to know what happened to his bride-to-be and to make sure she's safe. Don't shut him out when you need him the most. Give him the chance to be the man you dreamed of. Let him be your man."

Sister Girl nodded in consent to what her mother expressed and laid her head on Momma's shoulder. "I love you Momma. I love all of you." "We love you too," they said harmoniously with tears in their eyes. Sister Girl pulled out her cell phone from her jacket pocket to text Brother Man. If she called him and he heard how upset and shaken up she was, he would flip. So, she thought it was best just to text him:

"Hey baby. I hope I'm not disturbing you, but I really need you here with me right now. I'll tell you all about it when you get here. Please be safe. I love you." – {Send.}

At that moment, there was a knock at the door. "It must be the investigator," Ivory said. They all exited Sister Girl's room to greet the officer at the front door. Sister Girl answered the door. "Good evening, officer." "Good evening, ma'am. My name is Detective Blank. Our department received a call concerning a break-in at this address. Is that correct?"

"Yes sir."

"Are you the homeowner?"

"Yes sir."

"May I come in?"

"Yes sir."

As Detective Blank entered the home, he began surveying the damage. Due to his experience as being lead detective, he knew exactly what happened. "May I have your name for my report, please?" "Yes sir, my name is Sister Girl." "How long have you lived at this residence?" "Detective, I've lived here for four years and never have I experienced anything like this - ever." Sister Girl fought to hold back the urge to cry, but she didn't win the battle over her emotions. Her eyes began to swell with tears as Momma consoled her. "Sister Girl, do you have any enemies? Is there anyone that you believe will cause you any harm?" "No, detective. I have no idea who would want to do this type of damage or bring me any harm. As you can see, no material items were damaged in my home, only those things that held sentimental value were destroyed." Once Sister Girl spoke those words, Ivory remembered the picture frames in Sister Girl's bedroom. So, she rushed to retrieve them as evidence to the detective and jogged back to the living room. "Detective," Ivory addressed, "here are a couple of pictures that Sister Girl found in her room after the break-in."

While the detective viewed the pictures, Ivory continued, "The same dresses that Sister Girl wore in these photos are the same dresses that are now missing from her closet." "Was there anything else missing from your bedroom?" "No sir. I checked, and everything else seems to be in place." "Are you sure? Have you checked all areas of your bedroom?" Sister Girl noticed that Detective Blank was hinting that there was some doubt in his mind. "Detective, do you believe that something else may be missing?," Ivory asked. "I just find it odd that someone would go through all of this trouble to destroy your most memorable possessions and only take two dresses. Sister Girl, this home invasion seems personal. Let's check your bedroom again." At the detective's request, they all followed Sister Girl back into her bedroom. As soon as the detective arrived in Sister Girl's bedroom, he asked her to take a full inventory of her room. "Detective, as I mentioned before, I've already checked my room from top to bottom. There's nothing else missing." "Do you keep anything in your nightstands or dressers, anything of value?," Detective Blank asked. "Not really. Just my undergarments. My expensive jewelry is locked up in my safe. I don't have any—," Sister Girl stopped mid-sentence. "Wait."

She dashed to her nightstand near the window on the other side of her bed. She opened the drawer and began to panic. Everyone in the room could see her breathing becoming shallow. "What's the matter?," Coco asked. "My diary, my journal, all of my private thoughts and secret moments, my upcoming appointments and scheduled business meetings, wedding plans, they're all gone!" She was freaking out. She had to find them; if not, everything personal about her life will become public knowledge to whoever reads it. "Quick! Coco, check the other nightstand. Ivory, Candy, Momma, y'all check my dresser. I'll check the guest room." Without question, they immediately began the search as if receiving orders from a drill sergeant. After a couple of seconds of searching, "Any luck?," Sister Girl asked. "Nothing here," Coco said. "Nothing here either," Momma echoed. "What about you, Ivory? Candy, have you found anything?," Sister Girl panted as she dashed back to her bedroom. "I didn't find your diary or your journal, but I did find something interesting," Candy said in a curious tone. It was a handwritten note on a torn piece of paper that Candy found on the floor in front of the nightstand. "Oh no, that looks like a piece of paper from one of my diary entries," Sister Girl said in shock as she glanced at the note in Candy's hand. The date on the torn piece of paper was February 14th, the night of her engagement to the man of her life. Ivory glanced over Candy's shoulder just as she was passing the note to Sister Girl. "What did the note say?," Ivory wondered.

"It says - IT WILL <u>NEVER</u> WORK!"

Sister Girl slowly answered as she once again flopped onto the bed. Tears of depression and hopelessness fell from her eyes as she passed the note to Detective Blank.

Everyone in the room was able to feel the overwhelming feeling of despair as Sister Girl closed her tear-filled eyes and placed her head in her hands. "Why?," she whispered to herself. At that point, a whisper was the only thing that Sister Girl could muster. "Detective," Momma addressed, "please tell me there is something that you can do about all of this. Please tell me there's some justice for my baby." "I'll be the lead detective on this case, and I'll do everything in my power to make sure of it, Momma." He turned and gently placed his hand on Sister Girl's shoulder. "Sister Girl, I'm so very sorry for what has happened here. Please know that I will not stop until I have the suspect in custody. I'll take this note to our lab for analysis. If you have any additional information or evidence to provide, now is the time while it's fresh on your mind." Sister Girl replied softly, "Other than what I've already told you, and the fact that all of my keepsakes have been taken, I have nothing else to give Detective Blank."

Sister Girl took a deep breath, stood up from the bed, and headed into the hallway back to the living room. As everyone followed suit, Ivory remembered something. "Wait," Ivory interjected. "What about your crazy neighbor-friend that kept harassing you earlier today?" "Oh, yeah," Coco remembered. "That crazy woman came over here banging on the door, screaming, and hollering to the top of her voice. I tried to be cordial, but she wouldn't listen, so, I had to slam the door in her face," Coco reported to the detective. "Is this true, Sister Girl?" "Yes sir, it is." "How many occurrences did you have with your neighbor this morning?" "Several," she said as she rolled her eyes and shook her head in annoyance as she remembered what happened. "Have you had any occurrences with your neighbor prior to this morning?" "No sir, not personally, but she's known for 'throwing her weight around' when things don't go her way. Her dad is a 'big-shot' District Attorney, so she tends to hide behind daddy's 'persuasion'." "I see. So, explain to me what happened this morning," Detective Blank requested. As Sister Girl explained her crazy morning with the detective, Momma couldn't help but recall the mysterious woman dressed in all black that was standing at the end of the driveway earlier this evening, but was there really a woman standing there? Was she losing her mind? Momma knew without a doubt that there was a woman standing there, dressed in all black, at the end of the driveway. She was not going crazy.

So, as if she needed reassurance, Momma decided to look out the window to pinpoint the "mystery woman's" exact location for Detective Blank's report. When Momma opened the curtain, "AHH!" She let out a glass-shattering scream as she ran back from the curtain. Her fear startled everyone in the room. "Momma, what's wrong?!" asked Sister Girl in deep concern as she ran to her mother's side. Momma saw the strange woman again. It was the "woman in black," only this time, she was standing right in front of the window. Momma was so spooked; she couldn't get the words to form full sentences. "Th-Th-There's - a wo-wo-woman st-st-st-." Momma couldn't get it together. Detective Blank ran to the window and opened the curtain but there was no one there. "What happened?" Detective Blank asked Momma anxiously. "What did you see?" "I-I-I...," Momma stuttered in fear. "Someone, please get Momma a glass of water," Sister Girl asked. Detective Blank slowly sat her down at the dining room table to give her a few moments to calm down. Ivory placed a glass of room temperature sparkling spring water in front of Momma. Hands trembling, Momma picked up the glass of water and took a couple of sips. She inhaled and exhaled several times to calm her heart rate down. In through the nose - out through the mouth.

After a few moments, Momma was finally able to regain her composure. "Detective, earlier this evening, the strangest thing happened. I didn't have the nerve tell anyone, but with everything that has gone on tonight, I believe it's wise for me to tell you. When I arrived from the airport this evening, I requested airport transportation to drop me off here to surprise Sister Girl. The girls were out enjoying themselves and celebrating Sister Girl's engagement. When I pulled up, I got out of the vehicle and the transportation representative helped me with my belongings. When I reached the front door, he drove off. After I opened the door and looked behind me, there was a strange woman standing at the end of the driveway staring at me. She was as stiff as a board, and she was wearing all black. I could tell it was a woman because of her body shape. She looked so mysterious that I wanted to hurry up and come inside. After I entered inside the house, I quickly closed the door and locked it. I looked out the window, and she was still standing there staring at the house. I wanted to call 911, but I thought that I would be overreacting.

After about an hour or so, I needed to make a quick run to the store, so I found Sister Girl's keys to her car and went outside. I made sure to turn off all of the lights before I closed and locked the front door behind me. I got into the car, put the keys in the ignition, put on my seatbelt, and adjusted the rear-view mirror. As I was reversing out of the driveway, I looked into the rear-view mirror to make sure that I was in the clear and there she was again, standing there at the edge of the driveway wearing all black. I was so scared! I didn't want to get out of the car, so I turned around to look out of the back window to see if she was still there, and she was gone. I hurried out of the driveway and drove off. When I got back from the store, the lights were on inside the house. That's when the girls pulled up."

"Dang, that gives me the creeps," Coco said. "If you ask me, that sounds like that crazy neighbor over there," Coco added. "What would give you that impression?" Detective Blank asked. "Come on now detective," Candy said. "You have got to be kidding me. Sister Girl's next-door neighbor comes over here early this morning, banging on the door, yelling and being disrespectful, and then all of a sudden, she's scaring Momma like she's in a horror flick, and then Sister Girl's house gets invaded. It sounds like she's trying to get Sister Girl outta here - open and shut case."

Understanding yet firm Detective Blank replied, "As lead detective, I have to investigate all evidence and testimony. I cannot make any assumptions. I have to weigh out all of the facts. Now, were any of you present during the time of the invasion?" In silence, everyone shook their heads 'no.' "Momma," Detective Blank addressed, "did you see anyone enter or exit the property at any time?" "No sir, I did not." He took a deep breath. "So, unfortunately, at this time your testimony about what took place this morning and earlier this evening is circumstantial. Give me a few days to gather additional information, testimony from eye- witnesses, etc. I should have an update for you by the middle of next week. In the meantime, Sister Girl, I suggest that you find someone you can stay with until all of this is resolved. Perhaps, your fiancé would be ideal. Momma, I suggest the same for you."

"Well, Brother Man should be here shortly. Thank you, detective." "My pleasure, Sister Girl," Detective Blank replied as he proceeded to the front door. "For everyone's safety, I'll remain outside in my car until your fiancé arrives." Sister Girl was delighted to know that Detective Blank was such a gentleman. She politely escorted him to the front door, but once the door was opened, the women stood stunned to see who was at the door.

"OH, YOU GOT SOME NERVE COMING OVER HERE AFTER YOU DESTROYED MY SISTER'S HOUSE!," Coco said loudly from the living room. "Coco," Ivory interrupted respectively, "calm down. The detective said that it's all speculation. We can't prove that it was her without further investigation." "BUT I KNOW SHE DID IT! I KNOW IT WAS HER! THE SUSPECT ALWAYS RETURNS TO THE CRIME SCENE!" "Coco, be quiet!" Candy warned forcefully. They didn't need any additional drama, especially at that moment. The longer Gem stood at the door, the faster Sister Girl's heart rate began to increase. "What are you doing here?," Sister Girl asked coldly while staring at Gem with a heated look. "Why all the hostility?," Gem said smoothly yet sarcastically as she twirled her hair around her pointer finger, seductively looking at Detective Blank. "I just came over to check on my friend?" "Friend?...FRIEND?! WHO ARE YOU CALLING A FRIEND?!," Sister Girl shouted in agitation.

Momma quickly grabbed Sister Girl by the hand and led her to the kitchen to calm down. Detective Blank became curious concerning the outbursts between the ladies. "Excuse me, ma'am," Detective Blank addressed the uninvited guest. "May I have your name and your relationship to the homeowner?" "You can have whatever you like Officer," Gem said flirtatiously as she slowly closed into his chest. Detective Blank, aware of her advances due to his history of being approached by fast women, quickly backed away to keep the conversation professional.

He cleared his throat and said, "Again I ask you ma'am, what is your name and your relationship to the homeowner?" Shamed by his refusal, she said "My name is Gem, and I'm the friendly neighbor from next-door." Coco was standing nearby and couldn't wait to say something about the "friendly neighbor" part of her introduction, but one glance from Candy and she changed her mind. "Mrs. Gem?," Detective Blank addressed. "Oh, it's MS." Gem wanted to make sure, immediately, that Detective Blank knew she was single and available. Unfortunately for her, he showed absolutely no interest. He didn't take a second glance at her - absolutely no attraction. "Ms. Gem, did you notice any peculiar behavior in the neighborhood or any disturbances at this residence this evening?" Realizing that Detective Blank was focused on his responsibilities of the present matter, she decided to pause her pursuit. For some reason, Gem now seemed to be more concerned about sneaking a peek of the chaos going on in Sister Girl's house rather than answering the question. Distracted, she answered, "No sir, nothing noticeable." Detective Blank replied, "Oh, I see, however, there were a few disturbances with Sister Girl this morning I understand?" Still distracted, "Nothing major," Gem said and shrugged her shoulders. At her verbal response and nonchalant body language, Detective Blank decided to open his line of questioning further. "Ms. Gem, where were you around 7:30 pm to 8:00 pm this evening?" "Home. I was home."

"You were home the entire evening?"

"Yes sir, the entire evening."

"I see. Is there anyone that can verify your whereabout's?" With a devilish grin, Gem replied, "Why? Am I a suspect now, Officer?" "No ma'am, just gathering information about what took place here tonight. So, please answer my question if you would. Is there anyone that can verify where you were tonight?" Agitated, she said "No, but I was here when another woman arrived here in an airport transportation vehicle. She got out of the car and came inside the house. It seemed like she had a key, because she didn't have to struggle to get into the house. She was carrying a two-piece Louis Vuitton luggage set."

During Gem's description of events to the detective, Momma and Sister Girl exited the kitchen and walked back into the living room. Instantly, Momma recognized Gem's face; it was the same female features that frightened her when she looked out the window not too long ago. "That's the woman I saw getting out of the transportation vehicle tonight," Gem said as she pointed behind Detective Blank. Momma's breathing pattern began to increase as she looked into Gem's eyes from a distance. It was definitely Gem that she saw at the window. As Detective Blank turned to see the position of Gem's pointing, he noticed a change in Momma's stance. She seemed frightened again, which meant only one thing to Detective Blank - Momma has definitely seen this woman before.

Curious, he turned around to continue his questioning. "Ms. Gem, you seem to be a woman who notices great detail. You were able to tell me the exact design of a woman's luggage set at night from the comfort of your own home. That's impressive." "Well, thank you, Officer. I have an eye for high-class fashion designs." "You're quite welcome," he said with a smile. She assumed her charm was luring him now. He actually smiled at her this time. In her mind, his smile had to count for something, but what she didn't realize was that

Detective Blank was still focused on solving this invasion of home privacy. He found her responses suspect and that's why he smiled. He could have cared less about how she felt about him.

"May I ask you another question?" "Sure, you may." "Ms. Gem, how is it possible that you're able to recognize the distinct design of a woman's luggage set at night in the driveway of the next-door residence, and even able to identify the woman carrying the designer luggage set but, for whatever reason, you can't seem to "notice" any disturbances or odd behavior this evening at the same next-door residence? Surely, all of the commotion from this vandalism peeked your curiosity. What were you doing?" Feeling as if she was being interrogated or cross-examined, she began to lose track of her mental capacity to speak properly. She began to mumble and stutter. She didn't know what to say without incriminating herself. "I umm…Well…I umm…Let's see…umm. What was I doing around 7:30 tonight?," she asked herself loudly, looking up into the sky as if she was creating an alibi. "I was umm…I was umm…," she didn't know how to respond. So, out of fear she decided not to answer the question at all and instead said snobbishly, "I believe I'll speak with my father concerning this matter. I will not give you nor Little Girl the satisfaction of incriminating myself."

"CORRECTION! IT'S SISTER GIRL!"

Coco yelled. She couldn't wait to release that last outburst. Detective Blank turned around to Coco and motioned to calm down by placing his finger in front of his lips and then lowered his hands as if he was quieting her tone. Coco knew exactly what he was saying. "Ms. Gem, I believe speaking with your father, at this point, is a very good idea," he said. Gem slowly looked at the expressions on all of their faces and, in the presence of the detective, she devilishly looked at Sister Girl and squinted her eyes. After a few seconds of staring at Sister Girl as if she's plotting vengeance, she flipped her hair, turned around and started to walk away as a black Maserati sped around the corner and pulled into the driveway.

Gem was intrigued by the richness of the vehicle and immediately made her way to the driver's side. "Only a man can drive a car like that," she whispered to herself as she approached. She was ready to press her charm on whoever it was in the car, not realizing that pressing in on this one will cost her some confrontation. When Sister Girl glanced outside, she became overwhelmed with a sense of peace. Her love had come to rescue her, but not before Gem tried to influence him otherwise. Brother Man stepped out of the vehicle dressed in his routine business suit attire, and Gem couldn't wait to pounce. She slowly slithered her way to

Brother Man's chest and placed her hand on his pectoral region, as Sister Girl spotted her from inside the house. Without hesitation, Sister Girl ran outside. She was furious. At this point, she was just sick and tired of Gem and the storms she's already created that night. She forcefully pushed Gem away from her man, walked up close enough to Gem so that she knew that she was fed up, and said softly yet sternly and unapologetically, "You got the wrong one. If I *ever* see, hear, or suspect that you are *anywhere* near my man again, you and I *will* have another meeting, but the next time I will *not* be this cordial. It's not a threat - It's a promise. This is your first and *final* warning. Now, walk away."

Gem was stunned. She would have *never* imagined such words and attitude coming from Sister Girl. Gem wanted to say something to make Sister Girl's blood boil even the more, but she knew that any further comments would only result into a physical altercation, a battle that she *knew* she would not win, especially with Detective Blank still present. So, she decided to just stare into Sister Girl's eyes in an attempt to threaten her before she walked away, but it didn't work. Sister Girl showed no signs of backing down. She stood strong in front of Brother Man and was determined to let Gem know that she wasn't scared of her nor her craziness. When she realized that she was losing the "staring contest," Gem made the decision to retreat from her failed attempts to intimidate Sister Girl. She rolled her eyes, flipped her hair, and started walking down the driveway.

As soon as she reached the sidewalk, she turned around only to see Brother Man holding Sister Girl in his arms. It was so apparent that he loved her. Their love was so tangible. The way he embraced her was the way Gem desired to be held. It triggered memories of her own failed relationship that ended a few months ago. She became overwhelmed with emotion, depression, loneliness, anger. A single tear drop fell from her eyes as she witnessed Brother Man stroke the face of his soon-to-be bride. At that moment, as if he could feel Gem staring, Brother Man looked up from gazing into Sister Girl's eyes and noticed Gem standing near the street. When she realized that he was looking in her direction, she wiped her tear, blew him a kiss, and walked away. "What are you looking at baby?" Sister Girl asked. "Nothing baby, nothing," he said as he kissed her ever so gently on the forehead. "Let's go inside so that I can talk with the detective and find out what happened." As they continued to walk up the driveway, Brother Man made one last glance to make sure that Gem was gone. He didn't want any more problems for his love. He didn't see her, but Gem saw him looking for her as she stood nearby. The fact that he made another glance wouldn't mean so much to an average woman, but to Gem it meant only one thing - Brother Man wanted her. "I always get what I want," she whispered to herself as she smiled mischievously and entered her home. In her mind, Operation Brother Man had just commenced.

-3-

The Morning After

Sunday morning couldn't get here quick enough for Sister Girl. When the alarm sounded at 8:00 am, as it always does on a Sunday morning, she realized that she survived the night - barely survived - but survived, nonetheless. Since the chaos of her Saturday night really didn't end until 3:00 am that Sunday morning, everyone decided to just stay and crash with Sister Girl. They were all exhausted and had emotional hangovers. To them, it didn't make any sense to travel to separate destinations when they had already made plans to spend more time together on Sunday. Of course, those plans were made way before the mayhem. "Alright everybody, it's time to rise and shine!," Sister Girl yelled throughout the house. "It's time to get ready for service. It's time to give God some praise!" "Ugh. Why we can't praise Him here?," Coco muffled while her face nestled in the pillow. "I thought you said that He's omnipresent." "He is." "So, since He's everywhere at one time, He can hear my praise right here while I keep my face in this pillow. Thank You Jesus for not being deaf to my praise this morning. Hallelujah."

"Girl, get up," Momma said as she went throughout the house pulling covers and flipping light switches as she did back in the day. "What if the Lord gave you that same response when you called on Him? What if He said, 'I don't feel like moving right now? She'll understand?" Momma always had a way of humbling someone with the Word of God. "The Bible says in Psalm 34 that 'I will bless the Lord at *all* times, and His praise shall continuously be in my mouth.' So, that means…" "Yes ma'am," Coco interrupted. "I'm getting up." Coco didn't want to disrespect Momma but, at that moment, she didn't want to hear two sermons in one day. Candy and Ivory overheard Momma giving her morning message and began to snicker softly to themselves. They knew that if they laughed too loud, Momma was going to come to them next. Brother Man heard what was going on from the living room. He slept on the couch near the front door as a watchman over the house. He wouldn't dare leave after the commotion that took place Saturday night, especially when the love of his life was involved.

When he heard Sister Girl's voice, he sat up in anticipation and waited until he saw Sister Girl coming out of her bedroom. He wanted to welcome her to another day with a true love's morning kiss. As she exited her bedroom and noticed him waiting for her, Sister Girl's entire face lit up with excitement. She could still feel butterflies in her stomach every time she saw his face.

Heart rate increasing.

Palms sweaty.

Nerves tingling.

They approached each other in the living room. It was as if they were in the house alone. There was no noise. No chatter. It was just the two of them as they gazed into each other's eyes. Nothing could tear them apart. She couldn't wait for the moment to say, "I do." "Good morning my love," Brother Man said smoothly as he caressed her face with his soft hands and kissed her ever so gently yet passionately on her lips.

Lost.

Weak in the knees.

She couldn't find the words to express what her heart was feeling at that moment. All she was able to do is shake her head in amazement while she wondered why she deserved such a man. She inhaled and exhaled. She closed her eyes and replayed his kiss in her mind. She smiled. "Good morning my love," she replied as her mind continued to float. "Did you sleep well, baby?" "Not really," she answered. "I wanted to be in your arms. I needed to be in your arms. I wanted to come to the living room with you, but I knew that if I moved an inch from that bed, Momma would've called fire from Heaven to consume us both." They both began to laugh. He enjoyed seeing her laugh. He loved the way she would throw her head back and giggle. She seemed so free. No worries. No drama. Free.

"Sweetheart?" He didn't want to ruin the time of laughter, but Brother Man had to share what was on his heart. "Yes, my love," she responded. Whatever concerned him, concerned her. "Baby, with everything that took place last night until this early morning, you were barely able to get any rest. You may have thought I was sleeping, but I heard you praying all morning. The reason I know is because I was up praying with you baby. You didn't drift off to sleep until around 5:00 this morning. Now, I know how much you enjoy service on Sunday mornings, and I know that you're faithful to your relationship with God. Your consistency with Christ is what has drawn me closer to Him and closer to you. I admire you so much. My concern is that, though you have rest and peace in God, you haven't had a peaceful or restful night physically. I know your love for the Lord trumps your love for me, and it should, but, baby, I'm asking that you please reconsider going to service this morning and stay home and get some rest. I'm not here to control your decision in any way. I just want you to hear my heart. I love you baby, and I don't want you to exhaust yourself." Her heart continued to melt with every word he spoke.

Once again, Sister Girl is speechless. "Oh, how I love you," she said as she placed one hand softly on his cheek rendering a sign of affection. "I constantly wonder what in the world have I done to have the privilege of sharing my life with you. There will never be another. Baby, I truly appreciate your level of concern for me, and the respect you have for my relationship with Christ, but, honey, it's a privilege to serve the Kingdom on Sunday. Yes, there was a *lot* of drama last night. and you're right, I didn't get much rest, but I made a vow to the Lord that I will serve Him every chance I get." He slowly dropped his head, saddened that she wouldn't re-consider. "But" she slowly lifted his head, "I promise that, immediately after service, I'll leave. No after-church-parking lot chit-chat. Ok?" She kissed him softly on his lips. He smiled. "I'll go home and freshen up and meet you at the church." She kissed him again, turned and walked away so that she could finish getting dressed for service. "Mmm mmm mmm," he whispered to himself. He loved to watch her walk away. She turned around and noticed him watching her as she headed to her bedroom. She winked as she blew him another kiss. He smiled. He thought to himself "She means more to me than she realizes."

Just as he was about to open the front door, she stopped in the middle of the hallway as if she forgot something. "Hey everyone," she shouted throughout the house, "I almost forgot. I made dinner reservations for us downtown. We'll all meet back here right after service." "I sho' hope that service isn't long this morning then, cause a sista' is hungry," Coco said. "Coco, you gonna be the *first* one at the altar. Now, come on here." It was hilarious. Everyone began to laugh, but Momma wasn't playing around. She was serious. Well, sort of. She realized that the night before was really hectic, so she couldn't be too harsh on them, but she still wanted to get her point across. Her motto is: "As for me and my house, we *will* serve the Lord." Even though it wasn't her house, her motto still applied. "We all have approximately one hour to get dressed and prepared for service this morning. Come on, now. We can't make Sister Girl late, so, Coco brush your teeth. We don't want the Pastor passing out when he prays for you. And stop all this laughing." "Ha-ha-ha," Coco said sarcastically. Momma couldn't help it. She burst out laughing, which triggered a domino effect on the whole house. It was such a pleasant sound. The sound of laughter after a nightmare. A merry heart always does the soul good like medicine, and Sister Girl always remembers that golden nugget when she's going through her obstacles of life.

After a while, they managed to pull themselves together to remain on task. But they laughed almost ten minutes, which was now shaved from Momma's one hour "Let's Go" alarm. When the laughter died down, they all realized the time. The women began dashing in and out of bedrooms and restrooms frantically, trying to make up from the time they lost. Brother Man bade everyone adieu as he rushed to the driveway. He had no time to waste. He had about a ten-minute drive home, which meant he didn't have a lot of time to freshen up, get dress and head to church. Time was of the essence, especially if he didn't want to hear anything from Momma. The clock was ticking.

About forty-five minutes later, Sister Girl and her guests were all dressed-up in their Sunday's best and ready for service. As they headed to the driveway, Ivory paused at the front door as if there was something in front of her that was blocking her way outside. "Ivory, what's the matter?," Candy asked as she gently placed her hand on Ivory's shoulder. The morning's atmosphere was refreshing but, judging by Ivory's facial expression, it wasn't so pleasant; something was troubling her. It was the same feeling she had when she was in the car Saturday with The Phenomenal Four. Something just didn't feel right last night, and it didn't feel right now. Her feelings didn't steer her wrong the last time, so maybe this is the right time to let them know what's churning in the pit of her stomach.

They all stopped and looked at Ivory with deep concern. "What's the matter, sis? What's wrong?," Sister Girl asked. "I know we don't have time for this right now, but I think it's best that I tell you what's going on." Sister Girl looked at her diamond-pearl watchband and noticed that they were ahead of schedule. "Go ahead, sis. We have a couple of minutes." "Well yesterday, when we all got into the car, I had this crazy feeling that I just couldn't shake, and the further we drove away from the house, the stranger and stronger the feeling became. It was like a hair-raising creepy feeling that something was going to happen, and, when we got back last night, your home was vandalized. I'm the feeling the same way now."

"Well, I don't believe that anyone would vandalize the same house twice, especially since the detective is investigating," Candy said. "But it's not the same exact feeling. This time, it's deeper. It's almost like a gut-wrenching twisting. It's painful." Ivory looked at Sister Girl with full sincerity and tears in her eyes. "Sis, I know that you don't want to disappoint your Pastor, but I'm begging you to please re-consider. This feeling I have is scary, but, what's making it scarier is the fact that I can't tell you what may happen or what time of the day, but it will happen when you leave your home. I don't like what I'm feeling right now, and yesterday, my feelings were right."

As tears continued to flow slowly from Ivory's eyes, Candy and Coco nodded their heads in agreement with Ivory. Sister Girl turned to her mother to see if she was in agreement as well. "Sweetheart, listen…," Momma said warmly as she held her daughter's hands, "I know that serving the Lord is a major priority for you. I understand your need to be in the House of God because He's been so good to you. He's brought you through so many struggles in your life, but, you know that there are times when He's good to us behind the scenes, and we miss it because we're looking for His goodness in familiar ways and familiar places. This time, I believe within my spirit that He's showing His goodness by using Ivory as a vessel to warn you. Now, you know I love to praise, I love to worship, and I love to hear a Rhema Word from the Lord, but I believe today He's warning you. Sweetheart, you should take heed and stay home."

Sister Girl looked at her mother. Then, she looked at Coco, Candy, and Ivory. She knew what they wanted her to do, not just by looking at their faces, but she could feel them. She even felt a tugging in the pit of her stomach as if it was confirmation that it was indeed a warning. "But...," she said. For some reason, Sister Girl felt a high level of pressure when it came down to the church and, if she wasn't there even for emergency purposes, she had a sense of guilt lingering in her mind. Serving Christ was freedom, but when it came to the church, it felt more like obligation than serving. Deciding whether or not to stay home from church was considered a difficult feat to Sister Girl. She was stuck. What should she do? If she stays home, will the Pastor understand? If she decides to go to church, how would her sisters and Momma feel? She didn't know what to do. She looked at Ivory with tears in her eyes and immediately felt the tugging again. She took a deep breath in and exhaled as she looked upon all of their faces once more.

"Momma, Ivory, Candy, Coco, I appreciate your concern, and your love for me. I don't take it for granted. Thank y'all so much for caring for me, and I know that what I'm about to say will not be accepted as well as I hoped, but I have to be honest. Without a doubt, I believe that the feeling I'm having from Ivory is real, but I also believe that it could be a trick of the enemy to keep me - keep us - from receiving what the Lord has for us this morning, so, I must press my way. I can't allow the tactics of the devil to detour me from serving God. What if I stay home and there's a miracle waiting for me in my press?" "Well, what if there's a *tragedy* waiting for you *because* of your press? What happens then, huh?," Coco said while her care for her sister began to flare into frustration. "I mean, you're always there for the church and for your Pastor, even when they're not there for you when you're going through things in your life, and you're going to possibly risk your life to serve people that care less about you. Come on, Sister Girl. Does that make any sense to you?"

Coco said what she had to say but believed that her words made no impact at all. Candy couldn't allow the moment to pass without sharing her heart. "Sis, listen. From the day that we met until now, your heart has been centered around Christ. Your every waking moment belonged to God. From the rising of the sun until the going down of the same, the Lord hears your voice. I know how much He means to you, but, just like Momma said, I really do believe that He loves us and protects us behind the scenes. Whatever decision you make, I'm behind you, but please be mindful that the devil doesn't like you and would love to see you suffer in any aspect of your life. What if your leaving doesn't bring an attack on you specifically but to someone closest to you?"

Sister Girl dropped her head in contemplation of what her loved ones had spoken. Inhale - Exhale. She looked down at her watch. Time was well spent. She needed to decide quickly. If she waited just a few minutes more, she would be late for service. Her mind began to race. She looked down at her watch again, and it seemed as though the second-hand was ticking loudly in her ears. Why was this so hard? "I love you, sis," Ivory said softly. "Sweetheart, have you made your decision?," Momma asked. Sister Girl hesitated before responding. "Yes, I've made my decision." She paused again. Inhale - Exhale. "I'll stay."

Everyone inhaled and exhaled in relief of her decision. "Y'all go ahead inside. I have to make a couple of calls." They all kissed her on the cheek before walking through the front door. Sister Girl walked down the driveway to her car and leaned on the driver's side door. Inhale - Exhale. She lifted her head to the sky and closed her eyes. "Lord, please forgive me for failing to assemble this morning." Tears began to fall. The thought of her disappointing God broke her heart. After her abortion years ago, she made a vow to the Lord that she will serve Him until the day she dies. Not attending service this morning, in her mind, broke her promise. The more she thought about the decision she made to stay home, the more she wanted to just get in the car and drive off to church. Her love for Christ was worth more than her own life. He's the giver of life, so, if He decides that today's the day she breathes her last breath, then so be it.

"I can't do this. I have to go."

Sister Girl was determined at this point. She was going to church, no matter what anyone else had to say. She knew that she was already late for service, but at least she would be in the House of God. Since she still had her purse and Bible with her, she opened the driver's side door of her car, got in and hurried to put the key in the ignition. She pulled out her phone and called Candy while putting on her seatbelt. "Hey sis. You still making calls? You've been outside for a while." "Candy, please don't say anything, ok. Just listen. I'm going to church. I can't help feeling that I'll be disappointing God if I don't attend service this morning. I'm already in my car. I'll see you all at the restaurant. Love you."

She hung up. "Sister Girl?! Sis?!..Dang it!" "What's the matter?!" Ivory asked. They heard the sound of the engine and her car screeching out of the driveway. "She's headed to the church!" Candy yelled. "WHAT?!" "She said that she felt like she was disappointing God because she's not in service!" "Let's go! We have to stop her! We have to at least try! I don't like this feeling! It's getting stronger! Please you guys! We gotta catch up with her!"

Ivory had never been so nervous and scared. She didn't know what was about to happen, but she was certain that something was going to take place. They all grabbed their purses and ran to Candy's car, got in and sped off. Their adrenaline was so high that no one double-checked to see if the front door was locked but, honestly, at that point no one cared. Sister Girl's life was more important. Material things, like her house, can be replaced, but her life could never be replaced. The pacing of their hearts was beating in their throats. "Please Lord. Please let us catch up with my baby. Please." Momma whispered to herself. She just wanted her daughter safe.

Thankfully, Candy knew how to handle the road well enough to speed through twists and turns downtown. It was approximately a twenty-minute drive to the sanctuary. As fast as Candy was driving, they should've caught up with her by now, but Sister Girl's car was nowhere in sight. In a panic, Coco called Sister Girl but there was no answer. "She couldn't have been driving that fast! She was only like a few minutes ahead of us. Are we going the right way?" Coco was eager to find her sister - they all were. "I followed the GPS, and it says that we'll be there in five minutes. Maybe she knows a short-cut."

Five minutes later...*YOU HAVE ARRIVED TO YOUR DESTINATION*. But wait! Where's her car? Coco slammed the car into park, they jumped out of the car and immediately started scanning the church parking lot for Sister Girl's car. Ivory began to shed tears. "She's not here. Her car isn't here. Oh my God!" "Calm down," Momma said. "We have to believe that she's ok." She had to be ok. Momma is supposed to walk her baby girl down the aisle. Coco called Sister Girl's phone again, but still no answer. All of a sudden, an overwhelming feeling shook them. What if Sister Girl was hurt - or worse? They continued to take inventory of the large parking lot, with hearts still beating heavily and tears beginning to swell in their eyes. There must have been at least five-hundred cars or more. How in the world could they locate her car in the host of vehicles before them?

"Why don't we all split up?" Coco suggested that two of them head to the East Wing of the parking lot, and the other two head towards the West Wing of the parking lot. "I don't think that's wise," Momma said. "We'll be out here forever searching for her car. Why don't we just go inside of the church to see if she's here or if anyone has seen her?" They all nodded in agreement. When they opened the doors of the sanctuary, they were greeted warmly by hospitality, given masks and hand sanitizers, and directed to their seats. The church was enormous. Before taking their seats, they began to ask members of the hospitality committee if they had seen Sister Girl. Some knew who she was but hadn't seen her, others had no knowledge of Sister Girl at all. As soon as they sat down, Coco's phone began to vibrate. She took her phone out of her purse and looked down at the caller ID.

IT WAS SISTER GIRL.

"OH MY GOD!," Coco screamed as she jumped up. "Praise Him sista! Praise Him!" A woman sitting next to her thought that Coco was having her own praise break moment. Nope, that's not what that was at all. "Hallelujah!," Coco said trying to play it off. She whispered to the rest of the crew that it was Sister Girl on the phone. They all grabbed their purses and headed towards the front doors of the church. "Hold on sis. Let me get outside," Coco whispered to Sister Girl on the phone. They already seemed strange coming into the church looking around oddly, sitting down for two minutes, and then jumping back up and she didn't want to bring further attention by speaking loudly. Yes, Coco was a loud one, but she also knew the boundaries of being respectful in the Lord's House. They finally reached the outside steps of the sanctuary. "OH MY GOD! Are you ok?! Are you hurt?! Where are you?!" Coco quickly put her phone on speaker so that everyone could hear Sister Girl's response. "I'm ok. I'm fine."

"Girl, don't you ever scare us like this again!," Momma interjected. Though everyone's heart was relieved to hear her voice, they still needed to make sure that she was okay. "Where are you, sis?," Candy asked with deep concern. "Well, I was on my way to church when Brother Man called me. He told me that he was on his way to church as well but wanted to make sure that we were all ok, so, I told him everything that happened at the house this morning with Ivory's gut feeling. He agreed with all of you. At first, I wasn't going to change my mind, but, as he continued to speak to me, and I submitted to listening, I realized that what he was saying to me actually made sense, so, I turned around and headed to his house instead. I mistakenly left my phone in the car, and that's why I didn't answer. When I noticed that I had missed calls, I called you back."

"You should've known that we were gonna come find you. We love you, sis. You had us worried for real," Coco said. "I'm safe in the bosom of Jesus and in the arms of my man. No need to worry." Momma took a deep breath in and slowly released the tension she felt concerning the safety of her daughter. "Since we skipping church, can we go eat now?" Coco always had food on the brain. Laughing, Sister Girl told her to hold for one moment while she called the restaurant to see if the time of their reservation can be pushed up. While Candy, Coco and Momma was headed back to the car, Ivory froze again. This time though, Ivory seemed confused.

"Something's not right. Something isn't right," she whispered to herself. Momma turned around and noticed that Ivory wasn't moving. "Wait a minute y'all. What's the matter, Ivory?" "Momma, something just isn't right. I don't understand." "What isn't right?," Candy asked. "I don't understand. If Sister Girl is safe and she's with Brother Man, why do I still have this strange feeling that something is about to happen?" "Maybe you're just hungry," Coco said trying to be comical. "Coco please!," Momma said. "This isn't the time for jokes. Can't you see that something is going on with Ivory?" "I wouldn't joke about this you guys. I hate having this feeling. If I knew how to get rid of it, I would. I'm not playing around. Something is about to happen." Coco, shifting to concern, replied, "Well, maybe it's something else that you're feeling, sis. Maybe you're nervous about something. You do have that major company meeting that you have to host in a couple of days. Maybe that's what you're feeling. Everyone is safe and accounted for, sis." Candy tried to convince Ivory that everything was ok. "NO! Something is about to happen!"

-4-

Life or Death

POW POW!!!

Suddenly, gun shots blasting!!

POW POW POW!!!

It was coming from inside of the church.

Screams!! Church glass shattering!! Car alarms sounding!! POW POW!! Screaming!!

"OH MY GOD!! RUN Y'ALL!! RUN!!" Just as they began to run, the church doors were kicked down with people running everywhere trying to escape the horror taking place on the inside!

POW POW POW!!!

More screaming!! Babies crying!!

"RUN!"

"LET'S GO!" Candy, Coco, and Momma all began to run as Ivory stood in place crying. She was so frightful that it stunned her movement. Candy ran back to save her sister. "LET'S GO! NOW! MOVE IT!" Candy had to shake Ivory a couple of times before she came to the realization that they were in the middle of a shooting. "I SAID LET'S GO! MOVE IVORY, MOVE!" They ran down the stairs, while others rolled down due to the rush of people fleeing. When they got to the sidewalk, they noticed that Momma was missing. "OH MY GOD! WHERE'S MOMMA?!" Candy turned around. She saw Momma. She was being trampled in the stampede of people running from the church! "Y'ALL GO TO THE CAR! I'M GOING TO GET MOMMA! GO!" Candy ran back to the church steps for the rescue.

POW POW POW!!

She finally had Momma in her reach. Despite the hundreds of people running over her, Candy was determined to get Momma out of there.

POW POW POW!!

Screams!!

Crashing of cars in the parking lot!!

"I'M COMING FOR YOU MOMMA!"

Bloody and bruised, Momma reached out her hand to signal for help. Candy caught a hold of Momma's weakened hands and pulled her up. Candy turned around, saw Coco, and motioned to pull the car around to the front so that they can just jump in and speed off.

POW POW POW!!

Candy quickly yet carefully placed Momma in the backseat of the car and ran to the passenger side door. Ivory sat in the backseat crying and shaken up. "FLOOR IT!," Candy yelled to Coco. Coco pushed the pedal to the floor and sped off. Ivory looked at Momma to make sure that she wasn't bleeding profusely and noticed that Momma was now unconscious. Ivory began crying again. "What's the matter!" "She's unconscious!" "IS SHE BREATHING?!" Ivory continued to cry. "IVORY, IS..SHE..BREATHING?!"

"Yes!" Candy immediately dialed Sister Girl from the built-in car phone, but it rang busy. Candy quickly hung up the phone and called her back. "Hey y'all. I'm sorry I had y'all on hold for so long. The restaurant is busy..." Candy interrupted. "SISTER GIRL, YOUR MOTHER IS BADLY HURT! WE'RE RUSHING HER TO THE HOSPITAL NOW!" "WHAT?! OH MY GOD! WHAT HAPPENED?! IS SHE OKAY?! WHAT'S GOING ON?!" "THERE WAS A SHOOTING AT THE CHURCH!" "WHAT?! OH MY GOD! OH MY GOD! OH MY GOD! WHERE IS SHE?!" "SHE'S IN THE BACKSEAT. JUST MEET US AT THE HOSPITAL DOWNTOWN. HURRY!!" "I'M ON MY WAY!"

Hysterical and nervous, Sister Girl began to cry as Brother Man rushed to the hospital. "Baby, calm down. She's going to be okay. Everything is going to be okay. Don't worry." "Calm down? CALM DOWN?! I can't just CALM DOWN baby! It's all my fault! It's my fault that my mom is being rushed to the emergency room right now! If I would have just listened the first time they warned me, this crap wouldn't have happened! If I wouldn't have left my house, they wouldn't have had to follow me to make sure I was okay! Ivory told me that something bad was going to happen, she just couldn't tell me what was going to happen, and I felt it too - I felt it. I felt it in the pit of my stomach. All of you begged me to stay home, but, me and my too holy and too righteous self, decided to ignore everything that was said and felt, and I left anyway. How could I be so stupid?"

The more she thought about the whole situation, the more it made Sister Girl feel guilty about her decision, almost selfish. Tears continued to flow down her cheeks, but Brother Man was right there to comfort her through her sense of guilt. With one hand on the steering wheel, he reached over to touch the love of his life on her shoulder and whispered softly, "Baby, don't beat yourself up over this. You did exactly what you felt was the right thing to do. You placed God first, which is the way Christ intended. You had no idea there was going to be a shooting. No one could have known except for those that planned this evil and the Lord. We believe that "With His stripes" your mother is already healed. So, let's pray and believe God and rejoice victoriously. Ok?" Brother Man always knew the right things to say to sooth her spirit. "Now, take some deep breaths and relax."

Sister Girl followed his instructions. She loved her some him. Now that he's in her life, she had no idea what she'd do without him. About twenty-minutes later, they sped into the emergency department valet parking deck, where they met Coco, Candy, and Ivory. They both jumped out of the car. Brother Man ran to the valet attendant to have the car parked, while Sister Girl ran to the entrance of the ER to meet the girls. They all embraced one another as if they were in a love huddle.

"What's going on?! Why are y'all outside?! What's going on with Momma?!" Candy was the spokesperson and tried her best to answer Sister Girl's questions as calmly as possible. "After we brought Momma into the ER, the receptionist told us that we weren't allowed inside the ER waiting area due to COVID restrictions but assured us that she was in good hands. Only one person is allowed to visit Momma, but that's only after she's been placed into an exam room. I gave the nurse my phone number to forward any updates but, unfortunately, I haven't received any updates as of ten minutes ago. The last update was when she was in triage. I also gave the nurse your name and number and told her that you were on your way."

"Thank y'all so much for taking care of my mom," Sister Girl said as tears filled her eyes. As soon as the first tear drop fell, Brother Man was right there to wipe it gently from her cheek. "With His stripes, remember baby? I truly believe that Momma is going to be just fine. She's resilient. By the testimonies she's shared with me, she's been through many trials in her life, but she's bounced back every time. So, this right here is just another added testimony to share that God is a healer; just breathe knowing that she's in good hands." Inhale...Exhale. Sister Girl felt a little bit lighter. She kissed her soon-to-be gently on the lips and headed into the emergency department.

"Hello, my name is Sister Girl, and I'm here to get an update on my mother. When will I be able to see her?" Sister Girl couldn't help but fidget while the ER receptionist searched the database for her mother's status. "She's actually been placed into exam room 777 down the hall to your right." "Thank you! Thank you so much!" Sister Girl received her visitor's badge and, without delay, began speed-walking down the hallway. Her heart rate increased with every single step, not because she was getting tired but because she was anxious. "Lord, please let her be okay. Lord, please." It seemed as though the further she walked, the longer the hallway seemed to appear. When she finally reached

Momma's exam room, she inhaled and exhaled again to calm her nerves.

She had to be calm for Momma's sake, but she was afraid. She didn't know what to expect when she opened the door. Was she going to be hooked up to tubes and monitors? Will her face and body be badly bruised? Will she need plastic surgery? *OH MY GOD!* All of these questions hit Sister Girl at the last minute, which made her level of nervousness increase tremendously. Her phone rang. It was Candy. "What's going on?" "I'm sorry. I'm just getting to her room now. I'll keep you posted." Inhale...Exhale. As she closed her eyes, the words of her love continued to echo in her mind... "With His stripes, she's already healed." The more she feasted on those words, the less anxious she became. After standing outside of Momma's exam room for a few minutes, she finally gained the courage to open the door slowly with her head down. The sight of her mother in excruciating pain would tear her apart, so she gradually lifted her head.

Tears began to form as she gazed upon her mother in the hospital bed. Bruises to her face and arms were the obvious signs of some type of trauma. She was hooked up to an oxygen mask to maintain her levels and, of course, an IV for pain medication, etc. "Oh Momma, I'm so sorry." Sister Girl slowly approached her mother's bedside and gently took her hand. Momma slowly turned her head towards her daughter and smiled. "Hey sweetheart, how are you?" Though she was weak, Momma still had to be momma despite of her current condition. She still had to make sure that Sister Girl was okay. "Momma, I'm sorry. This is all my fault. If I would've listened to you, all of this would've been avoided, but no, me and my rebellious self just had to listen to the craziness going on in my mind. I knew I should've listened to you. I know those people at the church don't really care about me. They only care about what I bring to the table - pimping my gifts and talents, anointing and availability for their benefit and for their profit. They don't appreciate me! They don't believe in me, but trust me, momma, I'm not going back to that church. I promise. Wherever you are, that's where I'll be."

After Sister Girl's venting session, Momma began to smile and giggle, coughing in between her laughter. "Momma, why are you laughing? I'm serious. I'll be by your side forever." Momma chuckled again. She knew that Sister Girl was just in a wave of emotions at that particular moment and really didn't realize that majority of the things she said wasn't going to happen. "You're never going to leave my side, huh?" "No, ma'am. I promise. Never." "Well, it's going to be really hard consummating your marriage on your honeymoon with me in your face." Momma began to chuckle again, and so did Sister Girl. The more they pictured it, the more they began to laugh. Although Momma was in a lot of pain, she didn't want Sister Girl to forget that she has a wonderful life ahead of her with the one she will soon call her husband. There's no better way to lift a heavy burden than to bring laughter into a dreadful situation. The Bible declares in Proverbs 17:22 that "A merry heart does good like a medicine...," and Momma believed it with all her heart. In the midst of their laughter, there was a knock at the door.

The doctor entered and was pleased to see Momma in high spirit. "I'm so glad to see you laughing. And, I see you have a laughing partner with you." "Yes sir, this is my daughter, Sister Girl." "Nice to meet you doctor. Thank you for taking care of my mother. How is she?" Ok, play time was over. Sister Girl quickly shifted the atmosphere. She had to know about her mother's health, which was way more important at the time. "Well, I've ran numerous tests and, other than some minor cuts and bruising, your mother will be just fine. There are no indications of any internal bleeding or internal injuries. She does have a minor concussion, however, there is no cranial damage. I'll be placing her on supervised bedrest for the next seven days, and I'll call in a prescription for pain medication and an antibiotic for the cuts. The bruising will heal on its own. There's to be absolutely no lifting over ten pounds, no driving, and no flying for the next seven days..."

While the doctor continued giving his discharge instructions, Sister Girl's mind wandered off to the awesomeness of God. She began to worship God quietly right where she stood. She heard all that she needed to hear. Momma was going to be fine. "Do you have any questions, Sister Girl?" She was lost in the presence of God for a second. "Huh? Oh, no sir, no questions. I'm just so relieved that my mother is going to be ok." "If I were you, I'll be grateful as well. Many patients were rushed here from that very same shooting, but they didn't make it." There was a song that Momma always played, and Sister Girl remembered every line of the lyrics. She began to sing to her mother, "Millions didn't make it, but I was one of the ones who did." Tears began to stream down their cheeks as they began to worship right there in Momma's hospital room. It could've gone another way, BUT GOD! The doctor stood in awe as he witnessed them worship together with the unbreakable bond of love between a mother and her daughter. "Well, I'll let the nurse know that you're ready for discharge. It should only take about ten minutes or so to get all of your documents together. It was a pleasure treating you today Momma. You're an amazingly strong woman." With her eyes filled with tears, she said, "I serve an amazingly strong God."

A few moments later, just as the doctor said, Momma was being placed in the wheelchair and transported to the emergency room exit where a warm welcome was waiting. When Brother Man saw his mother-in-law and fiancé approaching, he swiftly asked for the valet attendant to get the car. "I'm so glad to see you're ok, Momma." Brother Man loved his mother-in-law deeply. A horrific tragedy snatched his mother's life away some years ago, so the love he has for Momma was not just coming from a son-in-law but from a son. They all gently kissed Momma on the cheek as she smiled with tears in her eyes. She felt so blessed to feel the wind graciously caress her face. She closed her eyes, titled her head back, and whispered sweet words of worship to the Lord. The tears of joy and gratefulness that cascaded down her cheeks meant something to her. It could've gone another way - BUT GOD!!

-5-

The Confrontation

Two weeks later, Momma was better than ever. Her road to recovery was a bit difficult, especially since she's used to moving to the beat of her own drum, but she managed to make it through with the help of her daughter, Brother Man, Ivory, Candy, and who could ever forget Coco. They were all so grateful for Momma's recovery, especially Sister Girl. Her complete recovery came just in time for her to join Sister Girl and Brother Man for their engagement party. Because of the catastrophe at the church and the trauma that Momma had endured, the girls decided to stay over for another couple of weeks after the shooting to help out with everything. Sister Girl had plenty of room in her townhouse for all to sleep comfortably, so it wasn't considered an inconvenience. Since they all had great careers that granted remote accommodations, they used it to their benefit, but Sister Girl wasn't thinking about remote accommodations, work, church. Nope. All she could think about was the engagement party tonight.

She was so nervous. She was pacing the floor in the living room back and forth as if it was her wedding day. "Girl, calm down. It's just the engagement party. Don't freak out. All you gotta do is say 'Hey y'all, I'm getting married,' eat and come back home. Don't sweat it. You got this. I did say that we gon' eat, right?" Coco always had something funny to say to make you shake your head and wonder about the next thing that's going to come out of her mouth. "I know. I know, but I can't help it. What if I freeze up and forget what to say?" "Girl, if you can't remember three words, I'm...Getting...Married, then I'm gon' have to go into my secret prayer closet and pray for you honey, cause something is definitely wrong." "Yeah right. What secret closet do you have, Coco?" Candy didn't believe it one bit. "It's a *secret* closet, and that's why you don't know about it - duh." "Girl bye. If you do have a secret closet, then it must be holding a whole lot of secrets in there, and prayer ain't one of them."

"Shut up," Coco said as she laughed at herself. She knew Candy was telling the truth, but the thought of having a secret closet wasn't such a bad thing to Coco. She thought about it for a few minutes. She knew that someone was praying and, with everything that she's experienced on her vacation with Sister Girl, she might as well join the prayer wagon. In the midst of their laughter about Coco's closet, there was a knock at the door. Sister Girl went to the front door and looked through the peephole - it was Detective Blank.

"Good afternoon Detective Blank, what a pleasant surprise. Would you like to come in?" Sister Girl opened the door to invite him inside. "Good afternoon ladies. How are you all?" "All is well. Thank you for asking. What brings you by, Detective?" "I called and left a voicemail message letting you know that my investigation was complete. When I didn't receive a response from you after some days, I decided to come by and give you the results personally and to make sure that everything was ok over here." "I apologize Detective. A whole lot has been going on lately. So, how did the investigation go?" "Well, after questioning the few willing witnesses in the neighborhood and reviewing your mother's testimony, it is believed that the suspect is a female, however, at this time, we are unable to pinpoint who this female suspect is due to the lack of DNA, fingerprints, etc. that will identify her. The one thing consistent in this investigation is that every testimony points to the fact that this female wore all black on the night of the break-in, just as Momma described."

"See! I told you that it was that crazy girl from next door!"

Coco couldn't let it go. She believed that Gem was the culprit from the very beginning. "Well, there's no evidence to prove that the next-door neighbor was involved. Being a disgruntled or emotionally driven neighbor doesn't provide factual evidence that she's guilty. If you should come across any new evidence to prove otherwise, please give me a call as soon as possible." "So, what now? Is that it? There's nothing else that you can do?" "Unfortunately, Sister Girl, I can only keep this investigation open for another week. After that allotted time, I have no choice but to close the investigation." "So, what about my belongings? She destroyed priceless items that I held dear to my heart, not to mention my long pink chiffon customized dress that I was planning on wearing tonight for my engagement party. How is this fair? How could she just force herself into my life and disrupt the peace that I worked so hard to keep?" "No one said that it was fair, Sister Girl, and I really hope that we can find this woman for you. As for your belongings, create a list of items you're missing and see if your insurance will handle the property damage for you. Again, if you find anything, please let me know. I wish you the best. Oh, I forgot to tell you one thing - I'm also handling the investigation of the shooting at your church. I'm so grateful and relieved that you weren't there." "I am too Detective but, if I had been there, Momma wouldn't have been hurt."

"No, I don't think you understand," Detective Blank said. "By witness testimony, the shooter aimed directly at your usual seat in the church and opened fire, but instead there was another woman sitting there that Sunday morning. Unfortunately, she didn't make it. So, it appears that someone made plans to shoot you. Those bullets were meant for you, Sister Girl." Silence gripped the room. "Sister Girl, do you know of anyone that would mean you harm to this extent?"

Sister Girl was speechless. *OH MY GOD! What in the world is going on?!* "First the break-in and now someone's trying to kill me! No, sir. Just like before, I am absolutely clueless." "Well, please be careful. I suggest, once again, that you inform your fiancé of what I've just shared. I don't suggest that you stay by yourself. Perhaps you need to stay with him for a while. If not, please invest in some type of legal protection, and please be careful. I apologize for ruining your evening, but I just thought you needed to know." With a revived overcast of sadness, Sister Girl gratefully replied, "Thank you Detective."

"Anytime."

Sister Girl sorrowfully closed the door behind him. Her entire mood changed because of what she just heard. Why this? Why now? Sister Girl didn't know whether to be shocked, scared or upset. She had mixed emotions on this one. Tears began to form, but right before she had the opportunity to sink into a deep depression, one of her sisters was there to the rescue. "Brush it off, girl! Come on now! You're here! You're alive! The devil tried it, and he failed - AGAIN! So, now it's time to Par-Tay! We have an engagement party to get ready for, don't we?" Coco started dancing - Go Go Go! Coco was shaking what her momma gave her, and Sister Girl couldn't help but laugh. Coco's intentions to make her feel better actually worked! "Alright everybody," Momma stopped the fun, "we only have a few hours before we have to leave for the venue. We have to make sure that my daughter is there on time. So, Coco..." Coco interrupted Momma. "Ha, I beat you to it this time Momma. I've already brushed my teeth." "Oh ok, but did you take a shower? I was about to tell you to stop waving your arms around like that. You killing the plants." They tried. They tried so hard to hold it, but they lost the challenge. Everyone burst out laughing, including Coco. Hysterical. "Oh, you got jokes huh, Momma? Ok, I got you."

After about a few minutes, Sister Girl realized that they were wasting time laughing yet again. "Ok y'all. We've got to focus. Time will fly by before you know it, and we won't be ready." Momma was just about to begin her time management speech, but everyone dispersed to their own quarters to get ready in a hurry. They didn't want to hear any speeches that day. Sister Girl thought to herself, "I love my family." Just then, her phone rings.

"Hey baby." Brother Man's voice melted her every single time. "Hello my love." Sister Girl's heart always skips a beat or two when she thinks about her man. His stature. His smile. His touch. His scent. His smooth lips. The unforgettable way he holds her in his arms. She drifted so far that she didn't even hear Brother Man speaking to her on the phone.

"Hello? Baby?" "Oh, I apologize my love. My thoughts were wrapped up in you. I can't wait to see you in a few hours," Sister Girl said. Her love sweetly replied, "I wouldn't miss this moment for anything in this world or the world to come. Just to gaze upon your beauty is what I've been longing to do all day long." He's done it again. She's weak in the knees, and he's nowhere near her. Inhale - Exhale. "Umm...," trying to focus her thoughts, "I have to go get dressed. I'll see you in a little bit." "Mmm, I can't wait." Sister Girl's eyes widened. Palms sweating. She bit her bottom lip. She definitely had to get off the phone, or she was going to forget all about the engagement party, forget about the rehearsal dinner and go straight to the "I do's" and the honeymoon. She cleared her throat. "Later my love." She hung up quickly, because if she heard him say one more thing, she probably would've hit the floor. She stood there in a daze for a few minutes still mesmerized by Brother Man.

SNAP! SNAP! "Girl, wake up."

Candy had to do something to bring her back to reality. She wanted to throw a glass of cold water on her, but every black woman knows that you do not, under any circumstances, mess with a black woman after she's gotten her hair done. Absolutely not. Out of the question. "Come on girls, let's move." Momma was on top of the time that they had left.

She was not going to allow Sister Girl to be late for her own engagement party.

After waiting about forty-five minutes, Coco, Candy, Momma, and Ivory were finally ready, but where was the guest of honor? "Sweetheart? You ready? We have to leave so we won't have to rush through the traffic downtown. Sweetheart, do you hear me?" Momma was wondering what was taking her so long. It's no big deal. It's just a party. Wrong. It may have been just a party to everyone else, but to Sister Girl this was deeper than anyone could ever imagine. This engagement party wasn't just about making her love known to her guests, but it was a declaration to herself that she has finally jumped the hurdles of depression, suicide, abuse, and loneliness. It proved that she's an overcomer. It was just as important as her upcoming wedding day, so, everything had to be perfect. She had to look her best tonight.

Because of tonight's importance, Sister Girl allowed nervousness to control the stability of her mind. Decisions, decisions. She tried on almost every dress in her closet more than once. She knew that she had to make a decision on which dress she was going to wear. *Ugh.* Sadly, her favorite pink chiffon dress, the one she wore on the unforgettable night that Brother Man proposed, was no longer among her choices because someone decided to be immature and vindictive.

Nevertheless, a decision had to be made. So, even though her heart wasn't in it, she had to settle with what she purchased last week. "Come on daughter." When Sister Girl heard the summoning of her mother's voice, she took one more glance in the mirror, slowly inhaled and exhaled, and exited her room. As she stepped into the hallway, the ladies smiled with love and awe. How beautiful! Sister Girl's face glowed. She was gorgeous. "Girl! Sis! Honey! You look amazing! You betta' watch out cause when Brother Man sees you, he may just take you straight to the altar...bump the engagement party." Coco may have said it, but everyone else agreed.

Honestly, Sister Girl wouldn't mind that at all. In fact, she already wished the same thing. She couldn't wait to be Mrs. Brother Man, but she really didn't want to rush through the bride-to-be experience. This was a dream come true. He was her dream come true, and she wanted to enjoy every moment. "Let's go meet my Mr. Right." As the ladies walked out of the front door towards her car, she couldn't help but wonder how he's going to react when he sees her tonight. Once again, Sister Girl was floating on cloud twelve. Nothing could break this incredible feeling of love bubbling over in her heart, until...

You have got to be kidding me! Seriously?!

Every tire had been slashed. All four! *This CAN NOT be happening right now!* Who could hate her this much? First, the home invasion. Then, the shooting. Now, her car. What's next? "Oh My God!" Before Sister Girl had the chance to freak out or shed a single tear, Candy grabbed her by the hand. "You don't have time for stress, frustration, or sadness right now, sis. Your man is waiting on you. I'll drive. We'll worry about this later." There was no doubt that the others were fed up with everything that had been going on concerning Sister Girl. In fact, they were beyond furious, and that's why they tried so hard to keep her focus on the happiness that awaited her instead of focusing on the chaos that seemed to take her life hostage.

Sister Girl closed her eyes as if she was shutting out the world and pictured herself in the strong masculine arms of her true love. Inhale - Exhale. "I'm coming to you baby." Her internal whispers brought about a sense of strength. Sister Girl was ready to push through. Whatever, whoever it was that was trying to kill her emotionally, mentally, and physically just lost the war. She refused to give up on life. She refused to give up on love. "This WILL NOT destroy me." She swallowed her tears. She looked at the ladies' faces and smiled with a heightened level of determination. "Come on my beautiful ladies. I have an engagement party to get to, and a man to kiss." After hearing the tenacity of Sister Girl, it was impossible not to give her kudos. High fives coming from all directions. "I know that's right, sis. Now, come on. I'm hungry." Guess who made that statement? YUP, the one and only Coco. Sister Girl looked at Coco with a smirk at first, but it quickly turned into a straight face. "Sis, I love you dearly, but, if you embarrass me at my party tonight, I'm going to hook you up with the ugliest and brokest dude there and, I will make sure that he has your personal cell phone number, your work number, your email address, your mailing address, your social media platforms..." Everyone started snickering as Sister Girl continued her list. "DANG SIS! You'll do me like that?" "Without hesitation." "Well, now that I think about it, go ahead cause A: You don't even know any ugly or broke men, and B: I know the caliber of company you keep. The ugliest man you know looks like a model on the cover of magazine, and the brokest man you know earns six-figures. So yeah, by all means, hook me up. Pleeeease hook me up."

    Sister Girl tried to keep a straight face, but once again, it was an epic fail; she couldn't help but laugh. Momma's heart was filled with an unexplainable warmth to see Sister Girl laughing. It was evidence that her daughter made up in her mind to move forward despite it all. "Come on, sweetheart. We have to go. It's time to celebrate." With much excitement, they all hopped into Candy's car, but Sister Girl had to make sure of one more thing before they left.

"Ivory, do you have any strange vibes right now? I made the mistake of not believing you the last time, and it almost costed my mother's life. I'm so sorry for taking your gift for granted." "It's ok, sis. I had never experienced anything like this before I came here to visit you, but, I have no regrets because it gives me the ability to protect everyone in a sense, or at least warn you. And, to answer your question, no. No strange vibes. We're good to go." "Thanks, sis." An instant smile appeared on Ivory's face after hearing Sister Girl's words. It meant a lot to Ivory that Sister Girl apologized to her, and then thanked her.

She always admired Sister Girl for her strength and humility. Even in her weakness, she seemed strong. Even in her accomplishments, she was graceful and humble. To Ivory, Sister Girl was a role model. She felt honored to be able to celebrate such a grand occasion with her sister, especially since she believed she would never experience love like Sister Girl. She tried so many times in college, but each attempt for a blissful life of true love ended horribly. So, she gave up. After praying, hoping, and believing on a consistent basis that her dreams would become her reality, it shatters over and over again - Forget it. What's the use? Ivory never lost the desire to experience true love, but her self-worth and confidence dwindled every time she heard: "You're a nice girl, but you're not my type", or "I'm not ready for a relationship", or "If you lose weight, I may want to holla at you", or "I only took you out because I felt sorry for you."

So, tired of being disappointed and hurt, Ivory gave up all hope of being loved. Sister Girl was so lucky. She found Brother Man, or rather Brother Man found her. She envied her. Instead of her enjoying the throwbacks and sing-alongs in the car as they drove through the night life and city lights of downtown, Ivory stared out of the backseat window as she reminisced about her loveless life. A single tear dropped from her eye, and then she realized that she was in her own world. She didn't want to bring any attention to herself by not participating in the fun, so she had to get over the feeling of always being a bride's maid but never the bride. *"What kind of sister am I?"* Her internal thoughts of selfishness hit her like a ton of bricks. She felt horrible. It's supposed to be a time of celebration for one of her closest friends, her family, her sister, but instead of congratulating her, she's crying. Why? Because deep down, she was a little jealous.

The GPS interrupted her thoughts. YOU HAVE REACHED YOUR DESTINATION. Ivory spent the entire car ride thinking about herself. She had to shake this, and she had to do it fast. There was no way that she was going to be the one to extinguish Sister Girl's happiness tonight because of her ho-hum. As Candy pulled up to valet, Ivory quickly whispered a short prayer to herself. "Is everyone ready?!

Let's get this party started - Whoop Whoop!" Ivory shouted. Shocked, everyone turned to look at Ivory. She would have never responded that way. It was obvious that this was too much for Ivory to handle. She didn't know how to fake how she was feeling. She tried way so hard not to bring attention to her tear-stained face that it actually brought the unwanted attention that she was trying to avoid. "Sis, you ok? Have you been crying?" "Uh… yes. I've been crying." She had to come up with an excuse off the cuff fast, without making it obvious that she was about to lie. "I'm just so happy for you, Sister Girl. Brother Man is such a blessed man to have you in his life." "Aww, you're so sweet." Sister Girl hugged her and gave her a side-kiss so she wouldn't mess up her lipstick. Pheww, Ivory was relieved that Sister Girl believed her slight untruth, but Candy and Coco weren't buying it at all.

Inhale - Exhale. This is it. This is the night that she proclaims her love for the one and only to family, friends, associates, and enemies. Inhale - Exhale. She heard the smooth jazz playing from the venue as she approached the doors to the entrance. *"Why are you so nervous, girl? Get yourself together."* Sister Girl had to talk to herself. She chuckled to herself as she began to remember that she felt the same exact way when Brother Man introduced himself for the first time. The more she laughed at herself, the more relaxed she became. She slowly placed her hands on the glass knobs to enter into the glamorous ballroom where she will fix her eyes on her man - her Brother Man.

Inhale - Exhale. She opened the doors. Music playing. Camera's flashing. People cheering. The special welcome brought her to tears. It was a wonderful feeling. There were so many people present, but it meant absolutely nothing to her until her eyes beheld him - and there he was. Standing afar in strength, masculinity and in all of his sexy was Brother Man.

Respirations increasing.

Palms sweating.

Butterflies swarming.

Their hearts intertwined while their eyes and souls connected. The entire room became still as the guests witnessed and felt tangible love without a single touch between the soulmates. Closer and closer they approached, weakening in the knees with every step. It was only two days ago since they were in each other's presence, but it felt so much longer. Closer and closer they drew until they met in the middle of the ballroom. As a ballad of love played over their heads, they held hands, whispered sweet words of love, and engaged in the most passionate public display of love with a kiss. Brother Man gently placed his arms around the waist of his soon-to-be bride, drew her closer and held her in his arms of safety. "I've got you, baby. Never worry. You and I together, conquering obstacles and transforming our dreams into reality - together."

Tears cascading.

Hearts melting.

How is it possible that love could be so powerful that it has the ability to make one speechless? She loved him so much. "You will forever be my love." She believed that this was the perfect opportunity for expression. She asked the host for the microphone and escorted Brother Man to have a seat in the middle of the ballroom. Surely, Sister Girl was about to serenade the love of her life, at least that's what everyone, including Brother Man, assumed was about to happen. But not so. Sister Girl looked deeply into the eyes of her love. "My baby, my love, my man. This piece is dedicated to you. It's entitled **Lost** by Kirah, better known as Shakirah Green."

> *Where am I?*
> *I'm lost in You...Embracing the moments that I share with You.*
> *Lost without You...Your presence near me shifts the capacity of my thought patterns.*
> *Love so rich...so deep, has me floating in a speechless abyss.*

Warm, divine, indescribable.

How could I feel what I feel? Inhale, exhale...so right, so real.

Who am I?

My selfish identity weakens at the sound of Your voice... Yes, I'm listening.

Just tell me, and I'll be whoever You want me to be. I relinquish my control.

You've rocked the very foundation on which I stand. Once solid and now liquid in Your hands.

Hold me the way You wish. Your wish is my command. You're in my likes. You're in my wants.

My senses are opened to You. My imperfections seem perfect to You.

My mental ability can't fathom why You love me.

But.

You.

Do.

I do. I will. Whatever. Whenever. However. Yes!! Lost in You. Lost without You. I'm Yours.

— **Poetry by Kirah**

Jaw dropped.

Palms sweating.

Pulse racing.

Heart yearning to hold her.

He couldn't believe that it was possible to love a woman the way he loved her. *What type of love is this?* She made his life complete. Whole. Nothing missing. He slowly stood to his feet, wrapped his arms around her waist, gently drew her closer to him. Cheek to cheek he whispered, "I love you baby, and I always will." A single moment. A single tear. She was his forever. Brother Man asked for the microphone. "Ladies and gentlemen, the woman that stands beside me is a phenomenal woman, a courageous woman, a virtuous woman, a strong woman, a woman of dignity, a woman of integrity, a woman of class and sophistication, a woman full of compassion, a woman of God. I have the honor and privilege of knowing her, loving her, serving her, and marrying her. Sister Girl has transformed my life in ways that I believed was impossible. She loves me in ways that redefines the definition of a king. God has truly blessed me beyond measure. There's no me without her." Brother Man turns to his bride-to-be and says publicly, "Baby, I love you so much."

With those words, a tear fell from his eye. She smiled as a tear falls from hers. A warmth saturated the entire venue and touched the hearts of all present. Such a sentimental moment. Brother Man and Sister Girl locked hands, looked into each other's eyes and - *Hold on.*

Wait a minute.

Why is Coco and Candy standing at the entrance of the venue? What's all the commotion? - *"You have GOT TO BE KIDDING ME RIGHT NOW!"* Brother Man drew closer to Sister Girl to keep her calm. "I'm sure they'll handle it, baby." He didn't want her going anywhere near the confrontation taking place. He had to make sure that she was protected at all times, especially since the shooting. Unfortunately, the main attraction was no longer Brother Man and Sister Girl's engagement, but instead it was the dramatic reality show taking place at the front door. The hostess ran to the door to move whatever the fuss was to the outside. Smooth jazz was still playing, so no one was able to really hear what was being said which was great - until the music stopped.

"I KNEW IT WAS YOU! I KNEW IT WAS YOU! YOU HAVE LOST YOUR WHOLE MIND SHOWING UP HERE! SOMEBODY CALL DETECTIVE BLANK!"

Coco was livid! The only one that had the ability to calm her down during her waves of anger was Candy, but Candy wasn't a good source of relief at the moment. She was just as angry as Coco. Ivory, usually the quieter of the Phenomenal Four, walked to the entrance way to see if she could assist with de-escalating the situation but, when she realized why Coco and Candy was so upset, her blood began to boil as well. "Baby, I have to go over there to see what's going on." "My love, I don't want you near that chaos, especially since everything that has taken place within the last month or so. Stay by my side, baby. Please." "My love, I appreciate your love and concern, but I have to find out what's going on. Baby, please. Whatever's happening right now has ruined our engagement party, and I need to know who it is. You can come with me if that would set your mind at ease."

Brother Man accepted her request and walked hand-in-hand with Sister Girl to the drama at the door. "I'm sure all of this is simply blown out of proportion," Brother Man said. He made every attempt to keep Sister Girl calm, until she saw what the fuss was all about. *"You have to be freakin' kidding me."* All she could do was cry tears of anger in silence. She couldn't believe her eyes, but there she was. Standing at the entrance of the venue in a beautiful long pink customized chiffon dress, posed with her hand on her hip as proud as ever as if she's done absolutely nothing wrong. It was Gem. "Congratulations, Brother Man. You're definitely looking amazingly handsome tonight. I can only imagine of how masculine you smell."

OH NO SHE DIDN'T!

Sister Girl's respiration rate began to intensify immediately, and her breathing immediately became out of control. She took a step towards Gem, but Brother Man refused to let go of her hand. Inhale – Exhale. Sister Girl turned around to look at her beloved in his eyes and said softly, "I'm ok, baby. I'm ok." He released her hand but still maintained his closeness. Sister Girl began to walk toward the female who destroyed her night. Where there was once peace, rage now occupied. She wanted to go off. To be honest, at that particular moment, she wanted to give in to what her flesh was telling her to do: *"KNOCK THE CRAP OUTTA HER!"* God will forgive her. He'll understand, but she didn't. She couldn't make a spectacle of herself. She's a woman of God and is not only representing the Lord, but she's also representing her future husband. *"It's moments like this that makes it hard to stay saved."*

She had to keep that thought within. Inhale - Exhale. Within a split second she found herself face-to-face and close enough to hear a whisper. Sister Girl stared with squinted eyes of fury. Calmly spoken, Sister Girl said "There are several things wrong with this situation, but there are also several solutions. Before I begin, I want to remind you of our brief yet vital conversation that we had a little while ago. If you recall, I told you that if I ever met you again in these circumstances that it wouldn't be as cordial as the first. I warned you that my words weren't threats but promises. Yet, here you are. So, since you're standing here, I can safely assume that you thought I was bluffing."

Gem's facial expressions and body language began to shift from confident to worry. "Problem number one: You have the nerve to show up to my engagement party when you weren't invited. Problem number two: No one knew of this engagement party nor the location unless you were personally invited by myself or my man. Neither of us invited you. So, how did you know? Problem number three: Not only did you show up to crash my evening, but you show up in *my customized* dress which was *stolen* from *my* closet when *you* wrecked my house. Problem number four: You're so easy, desperate, and trifling that you'll flirt with *my* fiancé while I stand in front of you." Gem parted her lips as if she was going to say something. "Shut your mouth. I'm not finished." Gem immediately closed her mouth, rolled her eyes, and sighed. "Now, here are the solutions. Solution number one: As a sign of maturity and accountability, you can call the police and admit to your illegal activity and wrongdoings; you'll save yourself the embarrassment and humiliation of being arrested in front of all these people. Or solution number two: *I* can call the police for you, Detective Blank to be exact, and notify him that we have the suspect in custody. You'll be handcuffed and escorted into the squad car while the world watches on every social media platform that I can find. You have two options. It's your choice. I highly suggest that you choose solution number one and show everyone here that you at least have an ounce of dignity about yourself. Otherwise, I'll have to choose for you."

Scared yet snobbish, Gem replied. "First of all, I care less about your problems and solutions speech, so, let's not waste any more of my precious time with that babble, shall we? Second, the only thing I'm guilty of is looking good and being rich, which is something that no one here can relate to. Third of all, my father is one of the most well-known attorneys in the country, so, if I *was* guilty of anything, which I am not, I wouldn't spend a second behind bars, and for your information, I didn't steal your dress. This dress was given to me as a gift. You're not the only one that has this dress, Little Girl. You can't prove anything. So, go ahead and call your little detective friend. I'm untouchable."

"There's no need to call me." Detective Blank began making his way through the crowd of witnesses. Momma called him when she first noticed the commotion taking place during the engagement party; she knew it would take him some time to get to the venue, and she wanted him to arrive before the situation got out of hand. Instead of her being outside partaking of the drama, she was inside of the venue praying and pleading the Blood of Jesus. Detective Blank began his line of questioning, beginning with Gem. "Ma'am, please state your name for my record." "My name is Gem, and I've done nothing wrong." "I see. Please understand that you are not under arrest. I am simply asking questions to bring about a peaceful resolve. Do you understand?"

"Yes sir."

"Now, from what I've heard thus far, it is my understanding that this party was private. Were you invited?" "Yes." "THAT'S A LIE!" Coco couldn't stand lies, especially the ones that were coming out of Gem's mouth. "Ms. Coco, I'm going to ask that you please refrain from interrupting." While rolling her eyes, Coco responded, "I apologize, Detective Blank." "Now, Ms. Gem, please answer the question. Were you invited?" "Yes. Yes, I was." "By whom, may I ask?"

"Umm…well…I umm…I don't know his name."

"So, are you telling me that you were invited to a private event by a man that you don't know?"

"Yes."

"Is this man here tonight?"

"I umm…I…I haven't seen him."

"I see. How is it possible that you could be invited by someone that's not even a part of the celebration?" Gem had no response, so Detective Blank continued his line of questioning. "Ms. Gem, you look beautiful. However, it is my understanding that you are now wearing the dress that belongs to Sister Girl. Is this true?" "No! This dress belongs to me! It was a gift. Little Girl is delirious. First, she accused me of breaking into her home, and now she's accusing me of wearing her clothing. I have *plenty* of money. I don't *need* to steal *anything*. I'm rich." Intrigued by her determination, Detective Blank replied, "I see. If this dress was a gift, who may I ask purchased the dress for you?" Gem seemed stunned by his question. She didn't know what to say. "Ms. Gem? Did you hear my question? Who gave you this dress?" "Well, I uh…umm…I don't know his name. But it's *my* dress! I have no reason to lie to you!" "Detective Blank, if I may interject." "Go ahead, Sister Girl." "All of my dresses are customized and tagged with my initials that are hand-stitched on the neck of each dress. I can recognize every single one of my dresses, and this one was very special to me, but now it's tainted by a criminal. If you check the neck of this dress, you'll see that I'm telling you the truth." Gem became extremely nervous. She had no idea that Sister Girl's dresses were tagged.

"Ms. Gem, please turn around with your back facing me and flip the collar of the dress so that I may examine the inside." Knees buckling, heart racing and hands trembling, Gem turned her back to Detective Blank and slowly flips the collar of the dress inside-out...but there was nothing there. No hand-stitched initials. Just loose threads. "Sister Girl, there's no initials visible." "I TOLD YOU!" Gem was relieved. "However, it does appear that someone has been tampering with this part of the dress. There are several noticeable thread endings here." "But, you have no proof, do you, Detective Blank?" Gem became very sarcastic, resembling the mannerism of her father in court. "Therefore, I'm free to go. You have no evidence against me." She was so sure of herself. She turned to look at Brother Man, winked her eye and said to him, "I'll see you later."

"Girrl..." Sister Girl was so ready to pounce, but she had something better up her sleeve. "Not so fast harlot. You need to stay to hear what I'm about to tell Detective Blank. I'm sure it'll be worth your wait." With sighing and rolling of her eyes, Gem decides to stay but only to continue lusting for Brother Man. Sister Girl noticed her advances toward her fiancé and begins to laugh. "You're so pathetic, and you don't even know it. My man is so out of your league. You can't play in these majors honey because I'm on all bases, and you just struck out. Now, get off my field." Yes, it's true that Sister

Girl's words were terrifying, but the look on Coco and Candy's faces enforced the terror of what would happen if Gem opened her mouth, so, she decided to be wise and kept her mouth shut. Thankfully for her, Detective Blank was there to keep Gem safe from any physical altercations.

"Sister Girl, did you have something to tell me." Detective Blank was trying to keep Sister Girl on track with what she wanted to say. "I apologize Detective, and yes I do have something that I would like to share with you. After you noticed that "someone" tampered with my hand-stitched initials, I remembered that there was something I hadn't shared with you before. I spent a great deal of money customizing this dress with little details that to others would seem insignificant and may not even recognize. For example, if you would look at the bottom of each sleeve near the cuff, you would see symbols honoring breast cancer awareness. Those symbols were placed on the dress in honor of my mother's fight against breast cancer." While Sister Girl was providing the emotional background history of her customizations, Detective Blank was following the storyline along with her on the dress. "If you would look closely at the seams within the layers of chiffon, you will notice a date. The date you see represents the month, day, and year that my father transitioned to be with the Lord. The four diamond-stud rhinestones on the satin sash going around the waist of the dress represents the Phenomenal Four, my sisters for life. Lastly, since I wore this same dress on the day Brother Man proposed, I placed the proposal date and our initials in gold embroidery at the base of the dress. I told you Detective, I know my dress. It's more than just clothing to me. It's memories."

Sister Girl became overwhelmed with emotion that she began to cry, and Brother Man was right there to console her. "Ms. Gem, you are under arrest for possession of stolen property." As Detective Blank was placing handcuffs on Gem, a tiny slip of paper fell from the sash around her waist. Sister Girl stared at the folded piece of paper laying on the ground as if she's seen it before. "OH MY GOD!" She bent down, picked up the piece of paper and began to unfold the edges. "Is everything ok, Sister Girl?" Detective Blank was concerned at Sister Girl's immediate outburst. "Detective, look! This piece of paper was torn from the journal that was stolen from my house, and that's how she knew about our engagement party! It has all the information written down. The date, the time, the location, even the dress that I was planning to wear, which is the one she's wearing now…it's all there!"

"Gem? Did you take a journal belonging to Sister Girl?" "NO!"

"So, how did you come into possession of a page torn from her journal?"

Gem knew she was going to sound absolutely out of her mind, but she had to defend herself since no one there was going to do it for her. "I know this will sound crazy, but it was the same man that gave me the dress and invited me to the engagement party. He gave me the slip of paper and told me that Sister Girl apologized for not formally inviting me." "Do you hear how crazy you sound right now?!" Candy couldn't understand how someone could have enough time on their hands to purposely attempt to sabotage someone's life. "Do you have a name?" Detective Blank needed to know in order to continue his investigation. "NO! I already told you that I don't know his name, but I promise you that I'm telling the truth. Look, Sister Girl, and I may not get along, and that's putting it lightly, but I will never stoop this low to damage her life. Why would I waste my precious time on her? I have no desire to invade her house nor steal her property. I have enough money to purchase her house, her clothing, and her personal property. I don't want nor do I need anything that belongs to her." Gem continued, but Detective Blank remained unbothered. "Well, you'll have plenty of time to think about what you're going to say to the judge on Monday morning."

"MONDAY MORNING?! I REFUSE TO STAY IN A DIRTY JAIL CELL FOR THE ENTIRE WEEKEND! DO YOU KNOW WHO I AM?"

"Yes, Monday morning, and yes, I know who you are, Ms. Gem. I'm Detective Blank, and I'm the law, and the law says you're spending the weekend in a jail cell." Sheer terror took over Gem's disposition as she squealed, "BUT I DIDN'T DO ANYTHING! I DIDN'T DO IT! I'M INNOCENT! I'M INNOCENT! I SWEAR!" Just as Sister Girl predicted, everyone's cell phone was out recording Gem being handcuffed and escorted to the squad car. Gem continued to scream her innocence until she was placed inside the vehicle. Amid all the commotion, Sister Girl remained in the strong arms of her true love. There was no other place she'd rather be, no other place that she could be, than to be with him. Brother Man looked down at the face of his beloved and gently wiped the tears that were flowing from her weary eyes. "Baby, I know that no one sticks closer to you than the Lord, but I make a vow to you right now that I'll never leave your side. As long as I have breath in my lungs, I'll never let you go." He kissed her ever so gently on her forehead as she held him tighter. "Please don't let me go, my love. Please don't let me go." Sister Girl, Brother Man, Momma, Coco, Candy, and Ivory all stood and watched Gem as she yelled from the backseat.

"You know her father is going to have her out of this mess with no jail time, right?" Coco hated to admit it but sometimes, unfortunately, money speaks louder than justice. "You know what, you may be right," Momma said, however, Galatians 6:7 declares 'Whatsoever a man sows, that shall he also reap.' The Bible also declares in Isaiah 54:17 that 'No weapon formed against thee shall prosper.' It may seem like she's getting away with the things that she's committed, but I serve a God that sits high and looks low. The Bible declares that He will bless those who bless us, and curse those who curse us. We're covered! Sister Girl is covered! My God is BIGGER than any problem, BIGGER than any circumstance, BIGGER than any obstacle, BIGGER than any diagnosis, and sho'nuf BIGGER than any demon, witch, or warlock. We're COVERED under the Blood of Jesus!" Momma always found a way to bring the Word of God to life, and everyone appreciated and honored the life of righteousness that she lives. Sirens blasting now. Detective Blank looked over at Sister Girl, signaled that he would give her a call and drove away. Inhale...Exhale. At least Sister Girl will have a good night's rest knowing that Gem has been apprehended. "I just hope and pray that this is the end of all this craziness."

-6-

Believe It Or Not

It's Monday and "Parting is such sweet sorrow;" sure, it's cliché from Romeo and Juliet, but it definitely fits the sadness and tears shared amongst Sister Girl, the Phenomenal Four and Momma. Because of the chaos that had been taking place, they all decided to extend their stay until the engagement party. They experienced so much these past few weeks, and everything that they went through brought them closer together as family. Departing seemed more like a "goodbye" than "I'll see you later," and even though Sister Girl and Brother Man's wedding was only three weeks away, they had no choice but to leave. Their personal lives were placed on hold and there were some necessary responsibilities that had to be handled. Momma had to return to Philadelphia to tend to a very important real estate deal that was about to close. Coco and Candy had to return to Detroit, and Ivory had to return to Atlanta. They all had to follow up on important business meetings and campaigns that they missed. Sister Girl understood because she, too, was behind in some major shifts that took place with her career.

Although she understood the reasons for their departure, it didn't take away the sting of saying "farewell until next time." Once again, tears began to develop into the corners of her eyes as she watched them drive away from her townhouse but, as always, Brother Man was right there to wipe every tear from her eyes. He made her a promise that he will never leave her side, and he meant every word of what he proclaimed to her. When her guests were no longer in sight, Brother Man held her close and requested that she stay with him.

"Baby, listen. Momma, Candy, Coco, and Ivory are gone now, and I don't want you here by yourself. The last few weeks have been absolutely traumatizing to you, and I cannot, scratch that, I WILL not leave my soon-to-be alone and unprotected. Come stay with me, baby, so I can make sure that you're safe." Lovingly but sternly, Sister Girl replied, "My love, I don't think that's such a good idea. Remember the last time I stayed with you? We came awfully close, extremely close, to engaging in some extracurricular activities." They both began to blush and chuckle. "I remember," he said as he began to reminisce and drift away. "Come back to me, my love." Sister Girl thought it hilarious that he drifted away so quickly just by remembering a moment that she spent with him. On the other hand, it wasn't so hilarious after all because a few seconds later, she began to reminisce and drift away herself.

The only thing that shook them from their daydreaming was the honk of a nearby vehicle. They both looked each other in the eyes and shook their heads in disbelief that it's possible to love so deeply. "Sweety, please stay with me. The thought of something happening to you rips my heart into pieces. I wouldn't want to live my life without you. I couldn't live my life without you. I have no life without you. Baby, please." Sister Girl searched his eyes and knew without a doubt that his words were coming straight from a place of love and sincerity. She had no reservations that his heart would lie to her. She knew him too well to think so lowly of her man. Often times, though, women succumb to a man's flattery and false innocence when she's in a very vulnerable moment. She was reminded of the time when she gave in to her previous fiancé and his fabrication of love, who not only broke her heart but broke her arm several times. So, to say "Yes" in a couple of weeks to the man of her prayers was an enormous leap of faith in love, but the way Brother Man made her feel couldn't be less than heaven on earth. Her "Yes" may be a leap, but it was one that she most definitely was willing to take. "Okay, my love. I'll stay with you."

Brother Man was so relieved that she accepted his offer. It wasn't the fact that she will be under the same roof before the ceremony that relieved him, it was that she will be safe so that there *can* be a ceremony. "Thank you, baby. Thank you so much. I don't know what I would do without you." Brother Man kissed her ever so gently on the lips. She smiled with the thought of kissing those lips all day for the rest of her life and being called Mrs. Brother Man. As they were headed back into the house hand-in-hand, Sister Girl's cell phone rang. It was Detective Blank. She placed the call on speaker so that Brother Man was able to hear any updated news that the detective was about to give. "Good afternoon Detective Blank. I have you on speaker phone so that my fiancé will be able to hear you. How are you?" "I'm ok, Sister Girl. Thank you for asking. Good afternoon Brother Man. Sister Girl, I have an update on Gem's arrest. I'm sure you are aware that her father is a very well-known and highly influential attorney in Los Angeles. With that being said, Gem's bail was paid on an emergency basis Saturday of last week, and she was acquitted of all pending and current charges early this afternoon at a private mediation in Judge's quarters. The Court ruled that the evidence presented was circumstantial and could not be used against her in relation to the crimes committed. Therefore, she was released."

"WHAT?! ARE YOU KIDDING ME?! SHE WAS WEARING THE EVIDENCE!"

Sister Girl was furious. The only other time she's been this upset is when her previous fiancé was found innocent on domestic abuse charges and released from custody. Brother Man tried to keep her calm, but this time was harder than before. "Baby, please calm down. I don't want you to have

an anxiety attack or stroke. Baby, please calm down."
"WHAT DO YOU MEAN CALM DOWN, BABY?!"

Sister Girl's head began to swirl. She started getting lightheaded and unstable on her feet. Brother Man quickly escorted her to the couch in the living room. "Baby, please. Calm down!" Sister Girl saw the desperation in his eyes and the concern in his voice. Inhale - Exhale. "Detective?" Brother Man interjected while sitting next to his beloved as she laid in his arms. "How is it possible to post bail on a weekend and, how is it possible to schedule a private mediation without the plaintiff *and* defendant present? Is that legal?" Brother Man wasn't an attorney, but he knew that two plus two wasn't equaling to four. Something was going on, and he wanted to find out.

"Off the record, Brother Man, I don't like this any more than you do. I've tried several different ways to find out how Gem's father managed to make such moves on her behalf, and I've still come to a dead end each time. I can't quite put my finger on it, but something doesn't seem moral nor ethical about this whole situation. Unfortunately, I can't allow my personal opinion to interfere with my professional outlook as a detective. The only thing that I can think of is…" Sister Girl interrupted Detective Blank in the middle of his statement, "Money! It's money! That's exactly what happened, and that's the reason Gem knew that she would get off as innocent when she was arrested last week. She's always prancing around bragging on her possessions and her wealth and how well-known her father is to the world of law. Honestly, it gets on my nerves, but, one day her arrogance is going to write a check that her daddy is not going to be able to cash. I mean, how could she ever be held accountable for her actions if she never has to pay the consequences?" "You're absolutely correct, Sister Girl, and what saddens me the most is that over the years, I've investigated many crime scenes that involved upper class individuals of all ages. Shockingly enough, *they* were the victims of their *own* crimes. Suicide is not just common amongst the impoverished, but amongst the wealthy as well. They seek pleasure from material objections, wealth, and the attention from others to fill a void in their lives that may seem like a permanent solution but it's only temporary. When they come to discover that they're lives are actually empty, they feel worthless and without meaning. So, in order to rid themselves of what seems to be a hopeless life, they decide to take it. Suicidal scenes are never easy to investigate. Gem could be using the "snobbish" act to fill the void in her life instead of suicide."

Deep breaths and sighs were audible from Sister Girl as she pondered the statements Detective Blank had made. She remembered those moments when she experienced suicidal tendencies. The feeling of hopelessness, helplessness, despair, and victimization was triggered from unpleasant encounters that she experienced from hurtful friendships and an abusive relationship. It was such a dark and lonely place to be, and she wouldn't wish that form of oppression and depression on anyone. "So, what now? What do I do? Is there anything I can do to fight this, Detective? She came into my home, violated my privacy, and stole my invaluable possessions. She can't just get away with that." "Sister Girl, unless you hire an attorney to perform extensive research into the legal handling of this matter, there's nothing you can do against the Court. There's a signed Order and Motion from the Presiding Judge that declares that Gem has been acquitted of all charges relating to this matter and was released with Prejudice, which means that it's dismissed permanently and cannot be tried again in Court."

Sister Girl shook her head back and forth in disbelief and anger. "UGH!" At that very moment, there was a knock at the door. Sister Girl got up from the couch and walked to the living room window to take a peek. She froze, but it wasn't because she was shocked. It was because, at that moment, time stopped, and she became as focused as an eagle zoning in on its prey. She spoke very confidently into her cell phone, "Detective, I think it's best that you make your way over to my house immediately, because there's about to be a confrontation that's gonna get real ugly real quick."

She hung up the phone. Sister Girl's response placed Brother Man on high alert. She's usually the one that's trying to keep everyone cool, calm, and collected. She's the Jesus Chick, but this time, he didn't see nor did he hear any type of Jesus coming from her. He became worried because he didn't want her to do anything or say anything that she will regret later. Not only that, he also didn't want her to incriminate herself by reacting based on her current mental state. When individuals react in an emotional state of anger or rage, unlikely behavior exudes louder than their common reputation. So, in a given state such as this, one can never say what they "won't do" because you never know until you're faced with a certain situation that you've never had to face. Brother Man jumped in front of Sister Girl to keep her from opening the door. Sister Girl looked at Brother Man in a way that made him think twice about getting in her way, but he knew that he loved her dearly and didn't want anything to happen to her so if it meant that she would be upset with him, then so be it. He didn't care how she felt towards him at that moment because it was dealing with her safety. He made her a promise, and he was going to do everything in his power to keep his word.

"My love, I know you love me, and I know you care, but I need you to please step away so that I can open this door." "Baby, you're absolutely right. Yes, I do love you and that's why I'm not moving."

KNOCK.

"Baby, please move out of the way."

"No baby, I'm not moving. I love you too much for you to belittle your character and fall into a trap of anger and blind revenge. You're not that woman." Sister Girl's agitation began to grow exponentially. Why did he have to be right? Dang it, man! He knew she was upset, too. He just cared more about her than her attitude. He looked at her with his beautiful eyes and winked. *"Dang, man. He makes me so sick, with his fine and sexy self"* is what she said to herself. Brother Man's rock-solid masculine image sometimes painted an inaccurate allusion, and that's what made her fall so deeply in love with him. To her, he resembled an exquisite morsel of rich milk chocolate. Firm on the outside but silky smooth on the inside. He winked at her again, and she began to melt. At that moment, all of the aggression seemed to dwindle away. He pulled her close and stared into her eyes. "You're bigger than your largest enemy."

After uttering words of empowerment to her, he kissed her ever so gently to let her know that she meant the world to him. KNOCK KNOCK. They both got so wrapped up in the moment that they forgot someone was standing outside the door. She looked at him, inhaled and exhaled, and nodded her head to let him know that she had everything under control. He politely moved out of her way so that she was able to confront Gem. She slowly opened the door. Sister Girl was ready for whatever sarcastic responses Gem was about to say. But, wait. Huh? Something happened, and it didn't make sense to her at all. Sister Girl was shocked. There she stood, with the stolen dresses draped over her left arm and Sister Girl's journal in her right hand. Tears and black mascara stained her face as she continued to cry. "Sister Girl, if you could find it in your heart, please forgive me. It was evil of me to wear your dress, especially one that means so much to you. It was evil of me to show up to your engagement party unannounced and uninvited. It was evil of me to upset you the way that I did. I sincerely apologize from the bottom of my heart. If you don't accept my apology, I will completely understand, but I hope that you will."

Sister Girl was stunned. She didn't know what to say. First of all, Gem *never* called her by her actual name. It was *always* "Little Girl." Second of all, Gem *never* apologized…EVER. All Sister Girl could do is look into Gem's eyes. "Please Sister Girl, please forgive me." Gem continued to cry in confession to Sister Girl. Something changed in Gem. There was a sincere brokenness. Not sure what transpired, but there definitely was a change, and Sister Girl felt it. She could see it in her eyes. "I forgive you." As soon as Sister Girl uttered those words, it was as if a burden had begun to shatter. "Gem, I forgive you." The burden became lighter and lighter. Gem was so grateful to be forgiven that she began to cry even the more. "Thank you, Sister Girl. Thank you so much. You have no idea how much your acceptance means to me." Brother Man began to smile. He was so proud of the way his love handled the situation. She could've been angry and bitter towards Gem. She could've kicked Gem her off of her property. She could've responded in many different ways, but she chose to show forth mercy. Honestly, with this display of integrity and poise, it made him fall deeper in love with the woman that took his breath away. "I know this may be a bit much to handle right now, but I couldn't allow the day to pass without me making things right with you, and, if you'd allow me to come in, I'd like to explain to you what actually happened."

Sister Girl paused for a moment. She didn't want to be too gullible. She needed to be wise. Just because she accepted her apology, did it mean she had to let Gem into her house? A few more seconds passed by and, as Gem stood at the door waiting for the invitation to come inside, Detective Blank's vehicle screeched around the corner. He sped into the driveway hoping to put a halt to any physical altercations between Sister Girl and whomever she was referring to before she hung up the phone. When he jumped out of his vehicle, he realized that there was no altercation at all, in fact, it was the complete opposite of what he was expecting.

"Is everything okay here?" Detective Blank looked at Gem's face and noticed the puffiness and deep red pigmentation of her eyes. He could tell that she had been crying hard for a while. But why? "Yes, Detective. Everything is fine. I'm actually glad you're here. I was just about to invite Gem inside." The expression on Detective's face was priceless. He looked just as confused as Sister Girl did when Gem asked for forgiveness. With a heart full of gratitude, Gem thanked Sister Girl for the invitation and slowly walked inside. "Here are your things." Gem extended her arms so that Sister Girl can take hold of her possessions. Sister Girl's eyes began to water as she reached for the priceless memories that had been returned. "Everyone, please have a seat. I'll be right back." With her dresses and journal in hand, Sister Girl walked down the hallway to her bedroom.

When she stepped into her room, all she could do is worship God, but just for a few seconds because she had guests waiting. She had to let Him know how much she loved Him, how much she adored Him, how much she appreciated Him. She was so grateful. "Lord, You lead. I'll follow." She didn't understand what was going on, but she promised the Lord that whatever the assignment, she would make herself available. This could be the moment that Gem gives her life to God, so she didn't want to stand in the way of a perfect opportunity. As she continued to worship, she placed her journal in the bedside nightstand where it belonged. Then, right before she was about to place the dresses on the bed, she held them close to her as if to say, *"I've missed you,"* but then something struck her attention. There was a scent coming from her clothing. A familiar scent. It wasn't a female's perfume. It was masculine. She's smelled it before, but couldn't remember when, nor could she remember who, but it was definitely a scent that she recalled. It wasn't her fiancé because his cologne has a smooth aroma. This scent was more of a dominant rugged aroma.

Puzzled, Sister Girl laid the dresses on the bed and headed back to the living room. Brother Man recognized the confusion on Sister Girl's face and asked if she was okay. She reassured him that she was fine and asked if anyone desired a beverage. After providing hospitality, she sat down and asked Gem, "What made you come by?" Gem inhaled and exhaled before she began. She didn't know if Sister Girl was going to believe her or not, but she had to tell her the truth. She had to take a chance. As she began to think about the way she's been treating Sister Girl, she began to cry again.

Sister Girl passed her a Kleenex and nodded to let her know that everything was okay. With tears in her eyes, she took a deep breath. "Sister Girl, I know that my being here may be awkward, especially after experiencing everything that has been going on for the past few weeks. I just couldn't let the day go by without letting you know how sincerely sorry I am for putting you through so much. If I could be completely honest with you, I couldn't stand you, and you know why? Because you have the life that I always wanted but never had. Yes, I have a nice car, a nice home and lots of money, but my life has so many voids. My life lacks so much, and I became extremely jealous of you. I envied you. You have a mother who loves you. You have friends who are like sisters to you. You have a man that adores you and worships the ground you walk on. You have a promising career and a lucrative business. You have it all, and I couldn't stand the fact that I couldn't have it too. So, my jealousy turned to rage and hatred towards you. Not because of who you are as a woman, but because of the life you live, the life that I wanted.

My mother and father divorced while I was in high school. My father would spend late nights at the office and tell my mother that he had to prepare for court and mediations, only to find out that he was committing adultery the whole time. It shredded my mother's heart into pieces. Even after the divorce, she still had problems dealing with the fact that her marriage was over. So, she distanced herself from me, and I haven't heard from her since that time. I'm an only child and, at that time, I had no friends to hang out with me. I had no outlet. So, I decided to become a snob. Why should I be the only one suffering in this thing called life? I might as well ruin everyone else's life. Misery loves company, and I was tired of being alone. Unfortunately, that behavior followed me into my adulthood. The sad thing is that I recognized the havoc I was causing, and I didn't care. So, when you moved here into the neighborhood and I saw your life and the love you received, I saw you as a perfect candidate but now I feel horrible. It makes me sick to my stomach to know that I've jeopardized your life."

    Tears of sorrow continued to flow from her cheeks. For a brief moment, there was complete silence. Sister Girl sat still in her chair, not knowing whether she should be offended or privileged that Gem would pour out her true feelings in an attempt to be free. "Wow. Umm, I don't know what to say. I mean, I know now why you treated me the way you did. But, why Gem? Why did you have to break into my home and take my most priceless possessions? I don't understand what type of gratification that would bring you." Gem paused. She had to prepare herself for how Sister Girl may react when she answered her questions. "I know that what I'm about to say may sound far-fetched to you, but I promise you that it is the absolute truth. If I've come here and poured out to you hoping to be forgiven, I wouldn't insult you and lie."

Gem inhaled and exhaled. "What I told you at your engagement party was the truth. I didn't break into your home. I didn't steal anything. Your dresses and your journal were given to me by a man that I've never seen before." "Please explain yourself, because yes it does seem far-fetched and I'm not understanding you right now." "Ok, listen. This may sound crazy to you, but just hear me out. A week or two before all of this chaos started, a mysterious vehicle pulled up in front of your house. It didn't park in your driveway, which was strange to me. It just parked on the street in front of your house. I wasn't sure if they were lost and needed directions or if they were stocking out your house. The windows on the vehicle were darkly tinted, so I was unable to make out a description of the driver. After a few moments, I decided to come outside to see what was going on. But, by the time I reached the vehicle, it sped off.

So, fast forward. Remember the day that your friends and your mother came to visit?" Sister Girl nodded her head. "Well, as soon as everyone left your house, the same mysterious vehicle pulled up again, but this time, they parked into your driveway. I was returning from my daily jog when I spotted the vehicle. I ran inside my house because I didn't want whoever it was to see me because it was just suspicious that the same vehicle would be parked in your parkway while you weren't there. By the time I got into my bedroom to look out of the window, the vehicle was empty. Seconds later, I saw your house lights turned on. I didn't think anything of it because I assumed you installed sensory lights that triggered upon some form of movement, but then, I heard some commotion going on inside of your house, which went on for about fifteen to twenty minutes." Confused, Sister girl interjected, "And you didn't think about calling the police?" With her head lowered, Gem humbly replied, "At that point in time, I didn't know what to do really. I remember thinking that it could be a domestic dispute that I didn't want to get involved in, so I decided not to call, but after the commotion stopped, I looked out of the window to see if I could see anyone coming outside. Unfortunately, all I heard was the car screeching away out of your driveway. So, I ran outside. Seconds later, your mother pulled up to the driveway. I didn't want to scare her by approaching, so I stayed my distance at the curb in front of your house."

"What were you wearing at that time?"

Detective Blank wanted to confirm the testimony that Momma had given. "I was wearing my jogging outfit. It was all black." Testimony confirmed. That's exactly what spooked Momma in the first place. Sister Girl heard everything that Gem said, but she still wasn't satisfied. She needed more. "I hear everything you're saying, but it still doesn't make sense to me. If you didn't break into my house, how did you end up with my possessions?" "This is going to sound weird, but it's the truth. Days later, after the break-in, a man knocked at my door. I never get visitors, so someone coming to my house was strange to me. I opened the door, and he handed me the dresses from your closet and the page from your journal. He handed me the page from your journal first and told me that you felt bad for not inviting me to your engagement party. He said that he was told to personally give me the page that listed all of the information concerning the venue, time, etc. He said he was told to let me know that you apologized to me for not formally inviting me, and then he handed me the dresses. He said, 'I think you'll look beautiful in these dresses,' and then he said, 'Especially this one,' and he showed me the pink chiffon gown. He told me to make sure I wore it to your engagement party. I haven't seen him since."

"Ok, wait. Back up. So, you mean to tell me that a mystery man in a mystery car broke into my home, stole my possessions, and then gave them to you? That doesn't make sense to me. Why would anyone want to do that, Detective?" "Unfortunately, many times individuals do things for the adrenaline rush and not necessarily for the material gain. It's actually more common than people realize. Many of the more memorable items that are stolen are either pawned or thrown away because it holds no sentimental value to them. Electronics, etc. are usually the items that are kept. So, I'm guessing that this man had no need of your belongings. He was just in pursuit of wreaking havoc in someone's life and, unfortunately, that life belonged to you." "It's still mind boggling to me how someone would go out of their way to target me like this. I mean, no, I'm not a perfect woman, but I know that I'm not a horrible one either." "And I didn't make things any better with my behavior."

Gem felt awful. As she looked at Brother Man and Sister Girl and noticed the love they shared and how they embraced, the feeling of shame hit her spirit harder than a Mack truck. "Sister Girl, if I may, allow me to also apologize for pressing myself onto your fiancé. It was rude, immature, disrespectful and unbecoming of a real woman. I may have my own 'violin story' and a list of personal reasons but, at the end of the day, it wasn't my place nor my man, and I'm really sorry to the both of you. Please find it in your hearts to forgive me."

She then turned to Detective Blank and apologized to him for her aggressive advances toward him. Given the testimony of her character from others, Detective Blank didn't expect anything less than the display that Gem put on that night of questioning. He had been in this profession for quite some time, and he recognized that Gem's behavior was only covering up something that she refused to reveal and let go. She's alone. She's scared. She's scared of being alone. She's lonely and desires attention of any form to help keep her internal sorrow at bay, but there was something different about this moment, something meaningful. Something special. Sister Girl, Brother Man and Detective Blank surrendered their forgiveness to Gem, at which time Gem began to cry in gratefulness. She cried not only because she was forgiven, but because she was surprised at her own behavior. Never would she have ever imagined being pulled in such a twister of vain emotion and bitterness due to the lack of love in her life. She felt horrible about herself, and about her life.

When Sister Girl saw the tears fall from Gem's eyes, a sudden quickening leaped within her. It was strange, but she decided to follow the lead of the Holy Spirit. "Not my will Father, but Your will be done." She slowly approached Gem, looked into her eyes, smiled, and extended her arms to embrace her. Gem, in the midst of her tears, was shocked. She couldn't believe her eyes, and neither could anyone else. She could feel her heart rate increasing. She could feel a tugging on the inside of her. She could feel an overwhelming feeling to pour out from her heart. It was a feeling she had never felt before. It was awkward to her, but she was so grateful that Sister Girl would take this time to embrace her instead of trying to get even. Gem slowly approached Sister Girl and mirrored her stance. She extended her arms to Sister Girl, and they both embraced. Immediately, something shifted. Sister Girl closed her eyes, lifted her head towards Heaven, whispered a prayer internally and then said something that no one expected. "Gem, I love you." At that very moment, there was a breaking that began to take place on the inside of Gem. She tried to hold it, but Sister Girl encouraged her to LET…IT…GO! Gem may not have known what was taking place, but Sister Girl did. Deliverance was taking place, and it was taking place right in her home. Though the men were quiet in this setting, they both understood what God was doing. So, out of respect, they decided to transition on the outside so that they could continue their conversation regarding the "mystery man" while God continued to have His way.

-7-

The Discovery

As the men were standing outside discussing the possibility of forming a plan to somehow get leads on finding this "mystery man," a strange vehicle rode by Sister Girl's house very slowly. The odd thing was that it didn't stop in front of Sister Girl's home. It stopped in front of Gem's home. "Brother Man, have you ever seen that vehicle before?" "No sir, I can't say that I have." Detective Blank wasn't in uniform nor in a police vehicle, so this strange vehicle had no idea that law enforcement was in the neighborhood. They both began to notice something peculiar. Though Gem didn't go into great detail about the "mystery vehicle," it seemed oddly coincidental and highly possible that this could be the very same vehicle that she mentioned. Detective Blank was too far away from the vehicle to note the license plate, however, he did make several notations about the make, model, and color, etc. After about a few minutes, the vehicle drove away. There was no horn blown, no engine raised, no speeding off. There was nothing done unseemly, which made Detective Blank even more curious. "Detective? Are you thinking what I'm thinking?" "I believe I am, Brother Man, I believe I am."

About an hour had passed and, since the men didn't hear the women travailing any longer, they decided to quietly walk inside and beheld a wonderful bond of friendship between Sister Girl and Gem. It was a miracle! Sister Girl was sitting on the couch as Gem laid her head in her lap. Remarkable! Detective Blank and Brother Man were amazed of how close they seemed to be now. Gem slowly lifted her head off of Sister Girl's lap and proudly proclaimed to Brother Man and Detective Blank, "I've accepted Jesus Christ as my Lord and Savior." A tear cascaded down her cheek. She looked new. She felt new. Sister Girl was so thankful to God for allowing her to operate as a vessel for the Kingdom, and to witness such an amazing life-changing moment for Gem.

"Congratulations Gem, and welcome to the Kingdom." Brother Man could see the glow of peace on his fiancé's face, and he was thrilled that she was able to free herself while assisting with freedom for someone else. Absolutely amazing! "Gem?..." Detective Blank wanted to get her attention. "Yes sir?" "Let me first congratulate you." "Thank you, Detective." "May I ask you an additional question? I know this may not be the best time, however, I believe you may be able to help me with this investigation." "Sure, Detective, anything I can do to help." "While Brother Man and I were standing outside a few moments ago, a vehicle slowly rode by and sat still in front of your house for a few minutes. Were you expecting company?" "No sir, not that I can recall. As I said earlier, I don't get visitors." "Well, do you believe you can remember the make, model, and color of the mystery vehicle you saw in front of Sister Girl's home?" "Absolutely." Detective Blank provided Gem with the information that he had written down about the vehicle that he and Brother Man just witnessed outside of Gem's home. As soon as Gem read Detective's notations, her eyes widened. "Yes, this fits the description of the same vehicle I saw in front of Sister Girl's home!" "So, does this mean that the same individual that possibly broke into my home is now plotting the same for Gem's home as well?"

Sister Girl needed to make sure that Gem wasn't in danger. "It couldn't be, because this is also the same vehicle that the mystery man got out of when he dropped off the dresses and the torn page from your journal." Something struck Brother Man's mind as they were discussing. "You know what? Come to think of it, I believe I saw this very same vehicle outside of the venue during our engagement party." "Wait! So, are you telling me that this person could be stalking me, stalking us, Detective?" Sister Girl became alarmingly concerned. "It's a possibility, yes, and, because of this new information, I think it's best that you, Gem, stay with your father, and you, Sister Girl, stay with your fiancé. I know I've suggested it before, but I'm no longer suggesting. I'm ordering you as an officer of the law. Leave this neighborhood until I can find out what's going on." "Well, I can't go to my father," Gem said. "After the case was over, my father told me that he only wants me connecting with him if there's money to be made. Otherwise, don't bother him with any other problems that are happening in my life. He doesn't want me messing up his reputation nor chasing off his carousel of women. So, it's a no go with my dad, but I'll find somewhere else to stay. No big deal. I have plenty of money, so survival won't be a problem."

Sister Girl looked concerned. "Are you sure you're going to be okay?" Gem looked into Sister Girl's eyes, held her hand and said, "I'll be just fine. I promise." They both smiled and nodded their heads to agree that everything was going to be just fine. "Great. Now that that's all settled, I need to head back to the precinct and refresh the investigation. If anything else takes place, or if you remember any additional information that will be helpful to this investigation, please let me know as soon as possible. Please remember this, if you should see this vehicle, DO NOT approach the vehicle, and DO NOT approach the individual driving the vehicle. Instead, give me a call immediately. Interfering can and WILL make things worse for everyone that is involved."

Sister Girl, Brother Man and Gem all gave their agreement to the instructions given by Detective Blank. As they bid the detective farewell, Gem also followed suit but not before exchanging telephone numbers and the locations where each other will be staying. Sister Girl closed the door behind Gem. When she turned around, Brother Man was right there. He wrapped his arms around her waist, pulled her close to his body, brush the hair from her face, and kissed her ever so passionately. She felt the warmth of his love trickle to her knees. It was hard to stand. It was liquid love from his lips to hers. Another unforgettable moment. "Baby, I've been waiting all day to hold you in my arms, to place my lips upon the sweet nectar of yours. Baby, I love you so much, and I can't wait to call you Mrs. Man in two weeks. I'm so ready to enhance your life with everything we've prayed and believed God for. I'm ready to allow God to do what He does best. I can't wait to be joined together forever."

Sister Girl began to cry. It's the only emotion fitting for this moment. Words wouldn't do justice for the way she was feeling when he uttered those words. With a voice full of love, passion, and warmth, she uttered the same. "I love you." Sweet, pure love. Brother Man believed now more than ever why God gave his Son, and why the Son gave His life. It was all about love. Deep, internal, eternal love. A tear fell from his eye as he began to thank the Lord for creating Sister Girl and forming her just for him. He gently wiped her tears, as she gently wiped his. They both embraced and showed their love once more through a kiss of passion. Hand-in-hand, they closed their eyes, and thanked the Lord together. Affection. Compassion. Hearts full of sincerity. They were made to be.

-8-

The Intruder

The days following were extremely tempting and difficult to overcome for Brother Man and Sister Girl. Though they respected one another to the highest degree, it didn't come close to suppressing the yearning they felt for each other. Yes, they're both saved, sanctified, and filled with The Holy Spirit and, truthfully, that was about the only thing that was keeping them from eloping. The fact that they couldn't jump start the honeymoon made it that more overwhelming, but, somehow their love, prayer and fasting kept them. Just as Momma would always say "the Lord will keep you if you want to be kept," her statement proved evident in this moment where they could've allowed their flesh to interfere with the purpose of their union. It was so much more than being physically intimate, it was about ministry. Brother Man and Sister Girl promised God on the night of their engagement that they will surrender their relationship to Him so that He can take control. They both had been hurt and scarred in previous relationships that weren't covered by the will of God, and they weren't going to make the same bad decisions again.

After following the instructions of Detective Blank, Sister Girl decided to move in with her Brother Man for the sake of her safety. So far, so good. Brother Man, being the gentleman that he is, prepared his room for his love and he took the couch. They made sure that they stayed apart as much as possible. They refused to give any key to the devil, especially since they're ceremony was so close. They were determined. One night though, it came really close...*really really* close. It was a night when they both decided to stay in and enjoy each other's company instead of being out on the town one Friday night.

Brother Man left the office early, purchased the necessary ingredients and scented candles, rushed home, set the table with white linen, candlelight, and a single rose. He then prepared one of Sister Girl's favorite dishes. When she walked into his condo, she was immediately welcomed by a passionate yet gentle kiss from her love. He relieved her of all of her belongings and hung her blazer on the coat rack near the door. He escorted her into the dining area where the delectable four-cheese vegetable lasagna, sauteed eggplant, garden salad and buttered croissant awaited her. As he seated her, he looked into her eyes and whispered, "I've missed you." At that very moment, Sister Girl only had an appetite for Brother Man. The meal would have to wait. She caressed his face gently and replied the same. Steam became more noticeable as they continued to gaze into each other's eyes. Brother Man stood Sister Girl to her feet, wrapped his arms around her to let her know exactly how he felt towards her at that moment. The atmosphere was instantly filled with love, sensuality, and a level of intense heat. Fire consumed them in seconds. They lost control of themselves as they indulged in the moment. Thankfully, Sister Girl's phone rang. It was as if the Lord used the mobile phone to stop something that could have brought deep regret between the two of them, and a dishonor to Christ. Since that Friday night, they both agreed not to allow their longing for each other to get out of hand. It was hard...man was it hard, but it was count-down to the big day. They believed they could do it. Just a few more days to go.

Brother Man and Sister Girl decided to take a couple of days off from work before the wedding. They didn't want to become overwhelmed with the frustrations of the workdays that they couldn't focus on their happiness to come. They wanted to be refreshed and prepared. So, on Thursday morning, a few days from the Saturday they would never forget, Sister Girl prepared a lovely breakfast for the love of her life and enjoyed a calm morning. They laughed. They reminisced. They daydreamed. It was a perfect morning. Unfortunately, their quality time was interrupted by a phone call.

"Hello." "Hey, Sister Girl. It's Gem. I apologize for disturbing you." Honestly, Sister Girl didn't want to be bothered, especially since she was laying in the arms of her man, but she promised Gem that she'll be there for her even if it was for just a few minutes. And, the way her morning was going with Brother Man, it was about to be a real quick phone call. "It's ok, Gem. Are you okay?" "Yes, I'm okay. Can you come over? There's an old friend that wants to see you." "An old friend? Who?" "I can't say. It's a surprise. How soon can you get here?" "Well, I was in the middle of something at the moment." "But they are really eager to see you." As Sister Girl began to listen to Gem's tone, she started to notice that her voice was a little faint and shaking as if she was nervous or had been crying. "Gem, are you okay?" "Yes, I'm fine. So, are you on your way?" Brother Man overheard the conversation and reassured Sister Girl that it was okay to leave and promised her that they will pick up where they left off. "I'm on my way, but I can't stay for long. I've made plans with my fiancé today." "Ok. I'll see you in a few minutes. Drive carefully. And Sister Girl, I love you." She hung up.

I love you?

Sister Girl and Gem exchanged those words often, but something didn't seem right. Sister Girl reluctantly grabbed her purse and her car keys. She looked into her love's eyes, not wanting to leave him, and said "I'll be back baby." Brother Man stood up from sitting on the couch and walked her to the door. "I'll miss you, my love." He kissed her. She smiled and closed the door behind her.

On the way to meet Gem, Sister Girl couldn't help but recollect how Gem sounded over the phone. The tremble in her voice was very noticeable, almost bothersome. Either she was telling the truth and was actually trying to keep this mystery person a surprise from Sister Girl, or Gem was lying and something was actually wrong with her. The one thing Sister Girl was definitely sure of was that Gem was nervous about something. She just hoped that whatever it was didn't ruin her day, especially when it could interfere with her quality time with her man. Besides, she's experienced enough drama within the last six months to write a best-selling novel.

Sister Girl finally arrived. The neighborhood was still quiet. No commotion. Her home seemed to be intact since the last time she was there, which was just a few days ago. She looked over to Gem's place and only saw her vehicle in the driveway, which was odd. Gem mentioned that there was someone here to surprise her. However, there was only Gem's vehicle in the driveway, so, Sister Girl got to thinking. Maybe it was Momma and the rest of The Phenomenal Four coming early to surprise Sister Girl. They weren't due to arrive until tomorrow evening, but they surprised her the last time. Maybe they've planned a repeated surprise attempt. If they flew in early, Gem could've picked them up from the airport and they were staying with Gem until she got there. *"But wait."* Sister Girl's brain was working overtime. Gem said "someone," which meant that it's only one person. So, maybe it's her mother. Excited, Sister Girl made her way to Gem's front door.

Knock Knock. She waited but there was no response.

Knock Knock. Still no response.

KNOCK KNOCK!

"Gem! I know you're in there girl! Unless you've decided to go somewhere by foot, you're here. Why are you hiding from me? Now, open this door child before I turn into the big bad wolf and blow your house down." Sister Girl started laughing to herself. She had grown fond of Gem, and their relationship had blossomed to a beautiful friendship. After a few seconds of silence, Sister Girl became concerned. She had just spoken with Gem moments ago. She knew that Sister Girl was on her way. She stopped her morning cuddle session just to come see the surprise guest, but Gem wasn't answering her door. Her vehicle was still in the driveway. Maybe she went for a late morning jog. Wait. That wouldn't make any sense. Why leave when she knew that Sister Girl was on the way? Sister Girl reached her hand inside of her purse. Dang it! She left her cell phone. Well, since she had no idea where Gem or this mystery person was and had no way of contacting her, she decided to head back to her place to check on things. There was no need to make a blank trip.

When she got to the front door, everything seemed alright. There were no signs of forced entry. No disruption of peace. All was well. She entered the living room and immediately smelled the fragrance of lavender and vanilla. One of her favorite home refreshers she used after cleaning. She closed the front door behind her. She dropped her purse and keys on the couch in the living room and headed to the kitchen to get a beverage.

"OH MY GOD!! NO! NO NO NO NO NO!"

Sister Girl was terrified. She slowly backed out of the kitchen shaking her head in disbelief. No No NO NO NO!

"I'm so sorry Sister Girl. I had no choice."

Gem felt awful. She'd never thought she would deceive Sister Girl again, but this time was different. "I had to. I had no choice. You gotta believe me," Gem said as she walked slowly out of the kitchen with a knife to her throat, hands bound together, and tears rolling down her cheek. "Please. Please don't hurt her." Sister Girl pleaded for Gem's life as she began to cry. "Come on now, Sister Girl. There's no need to cry - yet. I won't hurt her as long as you do what I ask you to do."

"Please. Just let her go. Please."

Sister Girl was desperate. She had to do something. She had to try. She made an attempt to take a step toward Gem, but the knife was pressed more firmly on Gem's throat, drawing droplets of blood. "STOP! Stop! Please!" Sister Girl shouted in anger and fright as Gem continued to cry. "Why are you here?! Why are you doing this?! Why won't you let her go?!"

The aroma of sarcasm filled the room. "Aww, how sweet of you to care. But, unfortunately for her, I'm not letting her go until I get what I want from you. Don't you see? Little Gem has played a major part in all of this chaos and drama, and she knows way too much, so, if I let her go now, it will only be to her grave. You wouldn't want that on your conscious, now would you Sister Girl? So, I suggest you play little nice girl so that Gem could live to see tomorrow. Okay?" When Sister Girl didn't respond due to her shock and fear, Gem's hair was yanked forcefully, scraping her neck on the blade of the knife. "Okay! Okay!" With eyes full of fury, they replied, "Good. Good. I'm glad you're seeing it my way. Besides, I could use Gem again. She's been extremely helpful. I have some *fun* things for her to do for me." "What are you talking about? What do you mean *again*?" Sister Girl was scared and confused at the same time. "Well, remember when she was trying to convince you that she was telling you the truth about a mystery man. You wouldn't believe her. You told her that she was lying to cover up her guilt. Well, guess what? Here I am. The truth stands before you."

"So, it was you?! You're the one that caused of this havoc in my life? HOW COULD YOU?!" He yanked Gem's hair again, clutching it into a ball in his fist. "Easy, Sister Girl, easy. Remember the fate of her life rests in your hands." Sister Girl had no choice but to calm down. She didn't want Gem to hurt any more than the level she was already experiencing. "Oh, Sister Girl. You're so predictable. You always have been. The same routine. The same secret hiding places. The same ol' boring life. You kept everything in the same places you used to keep them when you were with me. So, ripping your world apart was easy. Satisfying, actually."

He took a deep, satisfying breath as if to say that the way he saw this playing out in his head had finally come to full manifestation. "You surprised me, though. You escaped me at the church. Those bullets were meant for you. I could've stopped shooting when I realized that you weren't there, but then I saw some familiar faces. So, I figured since I couldn't get you, I'll target the ones closest to you, but they're still living, so my mission isn't completed yet. I still have some work to do, and that's where Gem comes into play." He looked devilishly into Sister Girl eyes and winked. At that moment, Sister Girl forgot that Gem's life was hanging in the balance.

The heat from her rage began to intensify. Her blood began to boil. To think that this psychopath almost killed her mother.

"MY MOTHER! WHAT?!"

Forget about the fact that he disrupted her life by breaking into her home and taking her most precious possessions, among other things. *"THIS NIGGA ALMOST KILLED MY MOMMA!!"* The more she thought about it, the more rageful she became. Her heart rate increased. Her breathing accelerated. Something began to happen. Boldness came from nowhere and it stood up strong within her like a warring lion. She didn't care what was about to happen to her nor to Gem, but one thing was for sure, Sister Girl wanted revenge. She knew what the Word of God said about seeking revenge, turning the other cheek and forgiveness. All of that is good, but for today — right now in this moment — she wanted him to suffer. Yep, she's saved, sanctified, filled with the Holy Spirit and on fire for God, but today was going to be that day she was going to have to repent. Something was about to happen.

Sister Girl looked at him boldly and unapologetically. She made sure that he understood that she wasn't backing down. She had a feeling that he was fueling his crazy based on the level of her fear, and she couldn't let him win. Not again. NEVER again. Sister Girl began to slowly walk towards him. With every step she made, he tightened his grip on Gem's hair which was still clinched in his fist. Trickles of blood became noticeable at the blade's edge as he held it tightly to her throat. Gem was terrified. She saw the determination in Sister Girl's eyes, and it didn't seem as though Sister Girl had their lives as a focal point. "*Not today. I don't want to die today,*" Gem whispered in her mind. She didn't know what Sister Girl was planning to do but, whatever it was, she hoped that it included her breaking free. Sister Girl noticed that Gem was losing her calm and wanted to reassure her that she was going to be ok. So, she looked at Gem and winked, which was a gesture that they used as a sign of reassurance – *We Cool*. Sister Girl continued pressing her way to him until the gap of distance between them was nearly closed.

"BACK UP NOW OR YA GIRL GON GET IT!"

Sister Girl knew that he was bluffing, and Gem knew that Sister Girl had absolutely no intentions of backing down. She's seen that look before and Sister Girl meant business, which made her even more nervous than before. Sister Girl winked again. Gem tried to calm down, but her mind and her body didn't get the memo. So, she closed her eyes to try and regain a level of sanity in the midst of this hostage situation.

Sister Girl looked him square in the eyes with no fear. She didn't yell at him, and she wasn't hostile. "If you wanted her dead, you would've killed her already. So, the way I see it, you need her. You're using her as your pawn to get whatever it is that you want. You're real good in manipulating people, especially women, by any means necessary which was the problem that caused you to get locked up. Now you're doing all of this. You went out of your way the minute you were released just to destroy my life and my family. I knew you could hurt me, but killing me? I wouldn't have ever imagined that you would stoop so low, but yet here we are in my living room witnessing a weeping hostage with a knife to her throat because you refuse to let go of something that you caused upon yourself. *You're* the one that couldn't be faithful. *You're* the one who decided to choose drugs over me. *You're* the one who decided to lose your temper. *You're* the one who decided to follow in your father's footsteps. *You're* the one that decided to ruin our relationship. Call it like it is.

Call A Spade A Spade! YOU GOT *YOURSELF* LOCKED UP!"

Tears of rage fell down Sister Girl's face, as she looked him eye to eye. "And now you have the nerve to come disrupting my life to prove a point! What point do you to have to prove, huh?! – that you jacked up your own life! You had great opportunities, but you decided to choose otherwise. How dare you come into my world because you obliterated yours?! You're pathetic. You make me sick."

Sister Girl's plan was working. He became angrier and angrier with every word she spoke. His chest began to rise and fall heavily and frequently, breathing heavy out of his nostrils like a sitting bull ready to attack. Oh yeah, she definitely hit a nerve.

"THAT'S IT! I'M TIRED OF YOU! I SHOULD'VE KILLED YOU WHEN I HAD THE CHANCE!"

He immediately launched at Sister Girl, pushing Gem out of the way! "RUN GEM, RUN!!" Gem took off running out of the house to find help! Back and forth! Back and forth they wrestled! She managed to knock the knife from his hand! He pushed Sister Girl to the ground hoping to pounce on her! She rebounded! She kicked his leg with all she had, knocking him to the ground! She tried to break away to her bedroom! She couldn't get up fast enough! He grabbed her foot, keeping her from crawling away! She grabbed a vase that was sitting on an end table in the living room! CRASH! She hit him on the side of his head, temporarily causing him to black out! Shattered glass everywhere! She ran to her bedroom to use the house phone! NO DIAL TONE! He cut the wires! Sister Girl started to panic! "*Think...THINK!*" She heard him groaning in the living room, which meant that he was coming-to. She quickly dashed from her room in attempt to run pass him before he got up! She was too late! He jumped up, grabbed her foot, and slung her to the floor! She violently fell to the ground, hitting her head on the arm of couch! She was out cold!

Tick-tock -Tick-Tock.

Brother Man didn't want to intrude on the love of his life, but he began to miss her. He wanted to wrap his arms around her and tell her how much he needs her in his life. He had plans to spend the entire day holding her, enjoying her, loving her, but, it's been about two hours, and he hadn't heard from her. She would always call him to let him know that she's okay and not to worry. It was like clockwork. Without fail. They wouldn't be apart for more than twenty minutes before she would call him. So, two hours was extreme. The more he thought about it, the more concerned he became. He picked up his phone and dialed her number. He heard music. Wait a minute, that sounded like her ringtone. *Dang it!* She left her cellphone. Brother Man became even more anxious. She couldn't call him because she had no way to call him. Wait, yes she did. He remembered that she had a house phone, but she hadn't even called him from her house phone. He called the house phone, but there was only a busy signal. His heart rate increased. Just the thought of something happening to her made him depressed inside. Brother Man got tired of playing investigator with himself. He had to find out if she was okay. With no more delay, Brother Man was out the door. He ran to his vehicle and sped off. The entire drive there, his fingers were clinched to the steering wheel. He tried deep breathing to calm his heart rate, but it wasn't working. It seemed as though he was in a warped zone.

"Oh God, please. Please protect her." Tears slowly began to form. "Please, Lord." He finally pulled up to Sister Girl's house, but something was wrong. Gem was standing in the driveway crying hysterically on the phone. He immediately parked his car and jumped out. "What's going on? Where's Sister Girl?" Gem tried so hard to tell him what was going on, but she couldn't formulate her words, only tears. Tears were her words. "Gem, what happened?! Where's Sister Girl?! WHERE'S MY WIFE?!" Still no helpful response. He grabbed the phone from her hands, hoping it was Sister Girl. "Hello?" "Brother Man, I need you to calm down." Detective Blank didn't know how much Brother Man knew about the situation, but he knew that Brother Man would try and resolve the issue himself. The outcome could end up in murder, and he didn't want his life nor Sister Girl's life ruined due to rage. "Detective, what is going on?!" "Brother Man, I'm on my way. Don't make any sudden decisions. I'm calling back up." "BACK UP?! BACK UP FOR WHAT?!" Brother Man looked at Gem once more. "Gem, Where…is…my wife?!" Gem nervously pointed to the front door. His heart rate dangerously increased. Pure adrenaline. Brother Man immediately dropped the phone to the ground and ran to the door! The door was locked!

Bang bang bang!

"Baby, open the door!"

BANG BANG BANG!

No response.

With all his masculinity, Brother Man kicked the door down! What his eyes beheld was a sight that he prayed he would never EVER see! The Lord ignored his prayer. The love of his life was lying on the floor motionless and unconscious, and the psycho-ex was straddled with his hands wrapped around her throat. Though there was no blood visible, all Brother Man saw in his eyes was red. "NIGGA GET OFF MY WIFE!!" He ran over to him and punched him so forcefully that it threw him off of Sister Girl! Brother Man hopped on him! *Blow after blow after blow!* He couldn't stop! He blacked out! His old nature was resurrected at the sight of his beloved laying on the floor, and he had no intentions of letting that psycho live! He wanted blood! *Blow after blow after blow!* His head was violently bouncing up from the floor due to the force of Brother Man's punches! Just then, Detective Blank ran inside!

"BROTHER MAN STOP! YOU GOTTA STOP MAN! HE AIN'T WORTH IT! THINK ABOUT SISTER GIRL! SHE NEEDS YOU!"

At no signs of stopping, Detective Blank ran and tackled Brother Man to the floor. Momma, Candy, Coco, Ivory, and Gem ran in behind the detective. They flew in early for the wedding. "NO NO NO NO! OH GOD, PLEASE! PLEASE!" They ran to Sister Girl with tears in their eyes. Momma knelt down next to Sister Girl and tried to remain calm. "Sweety, it's your mother. Please don't leave me. You have to fight baby. I need you. We need you." Momma's tears dropped and cascaded down Sister Girl's cheek as she laid motionless and barely breathing. Gem couldn't take it anymore. She ran out of the house weeping.

When Brother Man came to himself, he saw Momma kneeling next to the love of his life. He immediately began to cry. He crawled to her weeping. "Baby. Baby, talk to me." He noticed that she was fighting for her life, but it seemed like she was losing. With a great cry, "Baby please don't leave me!!" With no strength left, he dropped his head onto her chest and wept. "I can't live without you. I won't survive without you." Everyone stood around in shock. This can't be happening. Brother Man's sobbing and weeping for his love echoed and penetrated the house. Seconds later, the emergency response team entered the living room and saw that Sister Girl was motionless.

They quickly approached her and politely asked Brother Man to step aside so that they may begin emergency procedures to save her life, but Brother Man couldn't seem to pry himself away. "Sir, you have to move so that we can help her. We promise we'll do everything in our power to make sure she lives." Candy, Coco, and Ivory had to pull Brother Man away, while Detective Blank assisted Momma to her feet. They urgently checked her vital signs, which were thready, and her oxygen level was dangerously low. Suddenly, her heart stopped!

"NO NO NO NO! BABY, PLEASE!"

Brother Man screamed to the top of his lungs. This was a pain that he wouldn't wish on the worst of his enemies. The response team swiftly grabbed the defibrillator. "All Clear!" Sister Girl's lifeless body jumped. The sound of the jolts was horrifying to the ears of those standing and witnessing. *Flatline*. They increased the voltage.

"All Clear!"

Flatline.

"Nooooo! Noooo! Please God! Don't do this to me!"

Brother Man felt as if he was going to die if they couldn't revive her. He began to plead with the Lord in all sincerity. He was just about to spend the rest of his life with the only one that was able to make his life worth living. "Please God! Don't do this to me!" Brother Man's body lost every ounce of strength, and he dropped to the floor. He sat with his head in his hands and continued to weep as he heard the jolts of electricity. Sister Girl's body jerked with every shock.

"All Clear."

Flatline.

The response team took a deep breath in and out. Inhale. Exhale. They looked at Momma and shook their heads. A coldness filled the room. "We're so sorry. We tried our best. The time of death is…" "NO!" Immediately, a warrior rose up strong in Momma. "It ain't over until God says it's over and, if y'all don't have enough faith to believe that God can raise her from the dead, I need you to leave now!" No one moved. She instructed the response team to remain so that they can check Sister Girl once the miracle takes place. She walked over to Sister Girl's dead body, and she pointed her finger directly at her. With every ounce of faith within her, she began to declare, decree, and command her daughter's lifeless body to spring forth.

"FATHER, IN THE MIGHTY NAME OF JESUS, YOU DECLARED IN YOUR WORD THAT BEHOLD YOU HAVE GIVEN UNTO US POWER TO DECLARE A THING AND SO SHALL IT BE

ESTABLISHED IN THE EARTH. YOU DECLARED IN YOUR WORD THAT GREATER WORKS SHALL WE DO. NOW, WITH THE POWER AND THE AUTHORITY THAT YOU HAVE DEPOSITED AND ORDAINED WITHIN ME, I STAND AS A WOMAN OF GOD AND COMMAND MY DAUGHTER TO RISE UP FROM THE BED OF DEATH. EVERY DEMONIC FORCE, SCHEME, PLOT, PLAN AND ASSIGNMENT THAT THE DEVIL HAS CONJOURNED AGAINST MY DAUGHTER IS BROKEN NOW UNDER THE POWER OF THE BLOOD OF JESUS. I COMMAND EVERY DEMONIC SPIRIT AND DEMON OF DARKNESS TO RELEASE YOUR HOLD! YOUR VOODOO WON'T WORK HERE! YOUR WITCHCRAFT WON'T WORK HERE! YOUR SPELLS AND HEXES WON'T WORK HERE! YOUR DARK MAGIC WON'T WORK HERE! BECAUSE SHE'S COVERED UNDER THE BLOOD OF THE LAMB! SHE'S COVERED! SHE'S COVERED! SHE'S COVERED! SHE SHALL LIVE AND NOT DIE! SHE SHALL LIVE AND NOT DIE. TALITHA CUMI! TALITHA CUMI! GET UP DAUGHTER! SISTER GIRL, ARISE!"

Suddenly, Sister Girl's lifeless body began to twitch. Astonished, no one was able to move. All they could do is watch. The response team was amazed at the miracle they witnessed. She twitched again. And again! The response team ran over to Sister Girl and checked her vital signs. Her heartbeat was getting stronger! Her oxygen level began to increase! With tears in his eyes, Brother Man crawled to his love. "She's going to be just fine." All of a sudden, *POW!!* Brother Man immediately sacrificed his body to shield Sister Girl! Detective Blank looked down at his gun holster. His gun was missing! They looked around. Unfortunately, no one was paying any attention to the other body that was laying on the floor – the psycho. He had come-to, grabbed the detective's gun and pulled the trigger to finish the job. But it wasn't Sister Girl. It wasn't Brother Man. "AHHHHHH!!" Gem screamed in horror! "OH MY GOD! NO NO NO NO!" Momma was shot and collapsed to the floor, bleeding profusely from her abdomen.

Faint, but feeling accomplished, he replied with a smirk,

"I told you I was gonna finish the job."

...*To be continued.*

Author Shakirah Green

Loving, caring, compassionate, and, borderline comical, Shakirah Nicole Green enjoys expressing her God-given gifts and talents with the uniqueness of her character and personality.

Bursting out of her comfort zone was always a challenge for her but, one day, she made the determination to push passed her insecurities and said "hello" to opportunity. Because of her press, she's now the author of "Call A Spade A Spade" and "Brother Man, Sister Girl." Wife, mother, sister, Minister, and published author, we present to you, Shakirah Nicole Green.

www.ingramcontent.com/pod-product-compliance
Lightning Source LLC
Chambersburg PA
CBHW071719090426
42738CB00009B/1823